The A Judgment

Apostasy + Idolatry = Judgment

Dr. June Dawn Knight

TreeHouse Publishers

The American Judgment
@2020 Dr. June Dawn Knight
3rd Edition, #7 in the *We are the Bride Series*
This is the 3rd in the **American Quad**

For more information about the author go to:
www.drjune.org
www.wearethebride.us
www.watbradio.com
www.watb.tv

TreeHouse Publishers

www.gotreehouse.org

Printed in the United States of America

ISBN: 9798622912511

Introduction

Bride, I write this book very soberly considering what is about to hit our country. It is no laughing matter. God's judgment has already come. It has already started in many ways, but one morning we will wake up and the whole world will never be the same. The grid may go down, we may have no communications, etc. Natural disasters are already in crazy mode. I've never seen a year of crazy weather like we had in 2018. IT WILL GET WORSE. Now we have the "Coronavirus" and other plagues to follow.

As you learned in the previous books about APOSTASY + IDOLATRY will now = JUDGMENT. I believe we have went too far for the president of our country to repent and turnaround our country. However, if he would right now from the bottom of his heart and throws sackcloth on, we may experience a reprieve, but I highly doubt he will do this considering he was a part of the plan to begin with. The Bible has already foretold these events so our choice in this moment in time is our decision. I hope this book helps you to make better, informed decisions.

There is a purpose for judgment. We must consider that judgment is God's mercy. Sometimes we get stubborn and stiff-necked. God pulls his hand back and allows us to see and smell our own stench. A prideful church equals flattering prophets equals a prideful President equals a stubborn people. They're screaming peace and safety, but a huge tsunami is on the horizon. This group that has partnered with the Beast is telling everyone to take over mountains and that Jesus is not coming back until they take over the world. The deceit has reached every denomination and religion.

It has hit the masses. It is a mixture of religions, occult, worldliness and humanism. It is mystical and a hint of truth. The Bible says even the very elect "may" be deceived.

The only kingdom being setup now is the stage for the Antichrist. I hope to reveal God's heart about judgment and to reveal and highlight just some deceptions taking place.

We will also talk about the end of times and what does the Bible say about it? Where is our country going? What about us? What decisions do we need to be making right now?

As we close into Tribulation and the troubling days ahead, I pray this book prepares you to be the warrior that God has called you to be. Nothing that happens on the Earth is a shock to God. Nothing is too big or small for Him. He knows all and is all!

He has chosen you and brought your spirit to be here right now, for such a time as this. He knows what He is doing.

So, if He brought you here, then He can carry you here! He can help you to overcome and do whatever you need to do to fulfill your mission here on Earth. This is not the time to fear. This is the time to rejoice because our redemption draweth nigh. Time is running out and the enemy must be exposed so that we can reap the harvest for Our King, Jesus Christ.

We must be sober and alert and honest with God. We must also prepare our homes for what is coming and our families. We will talk about this.

We will examine the Book of Revelation as well. It's a fascinating book! We will talk about who God is. What is his heart? Why will he bring judgment? Be wise Bride! Jesus IS coming! Touch not the unclean thing! These are days of hope!

Job 19:29 Be ye afraid of the sword: for wrath bringeth the punishments of the sword, that ye may know there is a judgment.

CONTENTS

This book exposes the resulting judgment that is coming to the church due to the non-repentant church and nation. This book examines the Biblical standpoint on judgment and the church's role today.

The 1ˢᵗ book in the American Quad is called The American Exposé and it identifies the sickness in the church. In addition, it reveals the great apostasy so that the Bride can be well-informed. It exposes the devil's tactics within networks, politics, church, etc. It will clarify exactly what is the apostasy. It was revealed in 2017.

The 2ⁿᵈ book, The American Idols exposes the 40 idols that God brought before the 40-Day Team to address the throne. This team repented to God in the first 40 days of 2018. Once the church gets real with God, we can find true repentance. Unless you recognize the sickness, you cannot fix it.

The 4ᵗʰ book is The Last American Bride. This book recognizes the condition of the church and where we stand in this hour. Where do we go from here, and how do we prepare for the future? What about the mark of the beast? Martyrdom? All four books are the prepare the Bride for the days ahead.

1
A Refresher

In *The American Exposé*, I revealed the great deception. In this book I'm going to show you in greater detail, along with Biblical understanding of judgment. I'm keeping this within the American circle because I know my culture and peoples. I will be addressing many things in our country and exposing the enemy for who he is.

What is the Great Deception/Apostasy?
Apostasy + Idolatry makes it ripe for judgment!

As you read in the first book, the great deception is what the Bible terms as the Whore of Babylon or the Great Whore. This whore is a spirit or a giant who seduces the church and lures her away from the one true God. She seduces her into touching unclean things to gain more spiritual knowledge. She seduces her into the occult and New Age. How does she do this? She throws in a little leaven to leaveneth the whole lump. People say, "Just take the meat and spit out the bones." Well, you cannot find that anywhere in the Bible.

This whore is the Beast. It's one big spirit operating to pull the world together in one big unity for the cosmos/universe. Now with the Coronavirus, their campaign to pull the world in unity is called TOGETHER. You hear this word in songs, advertising, business meetings, Press Briefings at the White House, CDC, etc.

It's called The Ecumenical Movement. It is co-existing with other religions. It's wide-open and tolerant, inclusive of everyone. (Unless you're a fundamentalist – or traditional Christian – they will soon kill you! However, to everyone else you're welcome. Therefore, it is anti-Christ. It's for anyone who is anti-Christianity and anti-Jesus). The people that join this movement have jumped into a polluted river.

You know why? It's because God hates mixing! When you study the word of God and get to know him personally, you will see this. He is a jealous God!

I mean COMPLETELY JEALOUS! He couldn't stand it when Israel wanted kings. Why? Because God was their king. He walked with them, talked with them, and directed them intimately. It wasn't until his children wasn't satisfied with the requirements and boundaries set by God that they began seeking elsewhere. They wanted what other cities had (a king). They lusted after another. The same thing is happening today with this great deception.

> *Deuteronomy 6:15 – (For the Lord thy God is a jealous God among you) lest the anger of the Lord thy God be kindled against thee, and destroy thee from off the face of the earth.*

> *Exodus 20:5 Thou shalt not bow down thyself to them, nor serve them: for I the Lord thy God am a jealous God, visiting the iniquity of the fathers upon the children unto the third and fourth generation of them that hate me;*

Our people have become not satisfied with the tarrying, waiting, trusting, having faith, leaning, and walking with God. They want another king like the rest of the world has.

They want the extra-biblical knowledge. They want what the New Age has. They want what the occult has. They want the more. This is the Tree of the Knowledge of Good and Evil.

When we become a group seeking after signs, miracles and wonders, then we're in trouble. You say, "How do you know we are?" Well, it is obvious.

Are these same people in nursing homes, jails, prisons, on the streets, with the homeless giving out all this glory? Are they out with the ones who are hurting and GIVING IT AWAY? No! They are spending their hard-earned money going to another meeting to get this spiritual high and euphoria. Many of these leaders will say, "I get drunk and high on the Holy Ghost. Tokin' the Ghost. Drunk in the Spirit." Etc. This is a feeling and they travel anywhere to get more of it. This is part of that seducing spirit, which I identified in the first book as *Kundalini*. This spirit is from Hindu and New Age. It is a fake holy spirit. It is not the real one. This is the one with the manifestations of the "hippie spirit – goofy spirit".

These are the ones who look like they're high all the time but say they are in so much ecstasy with God's love and say, "Whoa man, wow. Woah!" etc. They look like they're literally hippies. There is an ora on them like people who are homosexual.

It's a look. They usually are effeminate-looking (skinny jeans, hair spiked up and shaved sides, v-neck shirt, tattoos, etc). It's a look of pride. They try to look "relevant and cool". For many of the women they have a spirit of lust on them. They wear short skirts, no sleeves, tattoos in hidden but yet visual places, colored hair like pink or purple, and some with revealing blouses.

3

It's no boundaries or modesty.

The manifestations also include jerking violently, laughing hysterically, growling, barking, etc. They stress the importance of gold dust, jewels, feathers, etc. It's unholy in all its ways. When you have discernment of spirits you can identify it quick.

In this book I will help you to go from here to the end of days. Many of you will die through martyrdom and many will die other ways or be caught up with Jesus when he returns.

Either way, just know that your time will not end without God granting permission. When you are his child, then your destiny is in his hands. The devil does not have a right to rob you anymore if you have shut all the doors.

I feel led to stop and say the sinner's prayer with some people who are reading this and don't know God. You need to make sure your heart is right with Jesus before you go any further in this book. The Bible tells us to examine ourselves. (1 Cor. 11:31-32). This book is for the end-time Bride. This is for the mature Bride who is ready to lay down her life for her king. If you are ready to lay down your life, then say this:

Dear Jesus, please hear my prayer today. Please forgive me for all my sins. I recognize that you died for my sins and rose again on the third day for me. I give you my life and I chose to lay down my life for you as well. I give you my whole heart. I surrender all. Please take these worldly desires out of my heart and help me to step into my destiny that you have lined up for me. I want to be all that you have created me to be. I renounce every agreement I made with the devil over the years. I am a child of God today. In Jesus' name, amen.

Congratulations brothers and sisters. You are now a part of the Kingdom of God. We must admit our need for Jesus. He is the only way to heaven! I also ask Holy Spirit to reveal himself to you.

We need to be filled with the Holy Ghost and power with the evidence of speaking in tongues to make it through the spiritual warfare we're about to embark into. We need this supernatural power. See, the Holy Spirit is a superpower within us (this is what I tell children when I minister to them).

He will teach us, guide us, instruct us, correct us, rebuke us, comfort us, etc. He will convict you when you sin.

He will confirm the word of God to you and you will begin to hear his voice and you two will make a great team. This is a gift from God to us to help us survive on this Earth. This gift of speaking in tongues is available to everyone. Here's a prayer for you to be filled:

Dear God, you sent your son Jesus to this Earth to show us our need for a savior and when he died on the cross and paid his debt that he did not owe, he instructed the disciples before his resurrection that he had to go so the Holy Spirit may come.

We know that you desire to help us all to be all that you have called us to be. Thank you that you sent the Holy Spirit to live on the inside of us and to equip us for our missions. I desire to have ALL that you have for me. I want it ALL. I want the fulness of you God. Please fill me with the Holy Ghost! I want your help in all aspects of my life. In Jesus' name. Amen.

Bride, the Holy Ghost is your helper. This is key for days ahead. This is a must. I'm praying in tongues now because I feel his presence all over me. I pray you feel Him too.

He is real and wants you to have all of him for this moment we are about to embark upon. Through this experience, you will step into the supernatural and not be led astray. Please understand Bride that we are not devoid of being deceived. The Bible says that even the very elect may be deceived. (Matthew 24:24).

It's pride that thinks otherwise. If you will pray every day, read your word and protect the gates into your home and heart, then you will be okay. I can hear some of you say, "Yeah, but look at those who are filled with the Holy Ghost and in the great deception right now."

True that, however I must remind you somewhere down the line a door was opened to the enemy and the deception came in. Therefore, we must shut all doors and gates into our lives. We must cast off all idols and shred the devil out of our lives. When we choose to hold on to something it keeps that doorway open.

Kingdom Now Connection to Luciferianism

Luciferianism is deeply rooted with the Masons/Freemasons organization. In that organization they are initiated into levels and when they reach level 32 and 33, it is revealed that it is Lucifer they're worshipping and serving. So, when we say Luciferianism, we mean the ruling spirit of the world. Lucifer will return as the Antichrist and the world will worship him. He comes as a wolf in sheep's clothing, which is why the New Age is pushing this "Another Jesus". They are reaching for this "Christ-consciousness" and leading the way for the New Age Christ to step on the scene.

It has infiltrated the church, and this is all partnered with the Ecumenical Movement. It ties with the Illuminati. The roots are the Catholic Church.

6

One of the head leaders of the NAR is Rick Joyner. Rick brags on his website about being in the Knights of Malta, which is a masonic group. I've spoken of him before, but now I found this woman that worked for Rick Joyner for years. She was deeply involved in his ministry. Part of her book title states – "One Woman's Deliverance from a Luciferian Gospel". She also revealed the connections to Kabballah and New Age.

The book is called *A View Beneath* by Michele McCumber. This is a MUST-READ book. You will be shocked at what she reveals.

As I'm completing my research, I'm discovering the connection between this Kingdom Now movement and the New World Order. If they are fighting to bring a kingdom on the Earth that is not God, then what kingdom are they preparing for their king? It must be the Antichrist, because what they're doing is not in the Bible and in God's timeline. When you read Jonathan Cahn's book, *The Oracle,* it makes it very clear their agenda about the return to Jerusalem and the Antichrist agenda.

The kingdom we're building right now is souls. Our main goal is to fight for individual deliverances and restoration to God. Nowhere does it say that we fight and climb to top of mountains, take control of the Earth and make the whole Earth Christian. No, the Bible says opposite. It says that we are to prepare mankind for his return and help souls to see the depraved world we're in and to make the right choices individually, not systematically.

Please hear my heart in that God does want us to pray for our cities and all that. I'm not saying that. What I'm saying is focusing our corporate efforts on building a worldly kingdom is not scriptural.

This kingdom and Earth have a destiny pre-written and we are to prepare individuals to choose right and to prepare to not take the mark.

While we are so focused on the seven-mountain NAR mandate and all this, souls are dying. People are over-dosing on drugs, etc.

If we have as much power as the NAR people say and they have all this dominion and control, then why not use it now and transform society? We are not here to heal systems…we're here to heal people to God. The Glory is all God's!

Back to Rick Joyner, In her book she states that out of the whole time she attended his church that they never opened the bible. She tells of a story of a man who came in one time who was reading his bible before service and they came in and carried him out.

In her testimony she states that the ministry often labeled fundamentalist and people who were of the "old order". She also wrote of many horrible things in which left her with the final impression that Morningstar Ministries is a Luciferian front.

She spoke of how witches visited his church every week and he spoke from the pulpit that they were welcomed there. But isn't it strange that if her story is true that the one who was reading his bible was not welcomed?

She continues.

"They arrogantly believe that it is only when they have conquered and subdued the nations that Christ can return. However, which 'Christ' are they building their New World Utopia for? If you substitute their use of 'Jesus' and 'Christ' for the word 'Corporate Christ' you have essentially the same doctrine as the New Age Movement and other Gnostic doctrines.

When most of today's evangelicals start agreeing with mystic, Gnostic, and New Age doctrine, we have a problem; a significant one. Dominionists preach another gospel and another Jesus; plain and simple." (McCumber, 2012)

Isaiah 14:12 "How you are fallen from heaven, O Day Star, son of Dawn! How you are cut down to the ground, you who laid the nations low!

Does this scripture not hit you hard? Consider Daystar television. Awaken the Dawn events led by Lou Engle, who is one of the heads of the apostasy.

Why Does the Apostasy Matter to Me?

The apostasy means that we're very close to the end of time. Most of the church is being lied to. We mostly need diligence and discernment.

When we examine the Old Testament, we discover how God tried to set boundaries with mankind from the beginning of time. He laid down the rules because he knows what it will take to have a relationship with him.

One of the main things we learn about God is how he hates mixing with other religions. He wants his people to remain pure and not touch the unclean thing. So, when his people start mixing and blending with the world, (Egypt), then God must back away because of who He is.

The apostasy matters to us because we must be aware of this plot so that we can protect ourselves and our family from the great lie.

9

We must resist and pull away so that we will not be deceived or sucked in. Through social media and the tendency to be concerned over likes and shares, etc., we can be pulled in our heart if people do not like us or disapprove of what we are doing. However, in this hour we cannot look at what other people think or do. We must measure everything by the word of God and truth and stick to it 100%.

It matters to us because it can send us to Hell. We can also send many other people to Hell as well. If we do not tell them the truth and they get sucked away, then their blood is on our hands.

Remember this Bride, the more we know, the more we will be held accountable to God. If God revealed it to us, then we must share with others so that they do not get sucked in with the lie either.

The apostasy is Satan's tool to take out humanity. This is the device he's using to take over the world in this new kingdom he's building. We must not help him. It matters because it matters to God.

What is the Idolatry in the Church?

Idolatry in the church is the 2nd book – *The American Idols*. In this book it reveals 40 idols in the church in America that we must tear down. Idolatry is anything we put in front of God. If we love it or that person more than God, then it's an idol. Remember that God is jealous for us and He wants no other lovers before Him.

It is important to get the idols out of our lives because when the Antichrist goes after us, we cannot allow a foothold to capture us. In other words, we do not want to give him an inch.

For instance, if we smoke cigarettes (which I used to and loved it), and we can't give them up to God, then when times get hard (economy crashes, natural disaster, war, etc.), then we may sell our soul for a cigarette.

Why Do Idols & Apostasy Hinder Me?

It hinders you because it is the enemy's plan to hold you back and not allow you to be all that God has called you to be. God has a plan for your life, and it will involve suffering and persecution. To preach and live the Bible in absolute truth, you will be persecuted! You will especially be persecuted if you go against the apostasy and the normal flow of society. Both will send you to Hell. Here are a few scriptures:

> *Leviticus 19:4 Turn ye not unto idols, nor make to yourselves molten gods: I am the Lord your God.*
>
> *Leviticus 26:1 Ye shall make you no idols nor graven image, neither rear you up a standing image, neither shall ye set up any image of stone in your land, to bow down unto it: for I am the Lord your God.*
>
> *1 Samuel 15:23 For rebellion is as the sin of witchcraft, and stubbornness is as iniquity and idolatry. Because thou hast rejected the word of the Lord, he hath also rejected thee from being king*
> *.*
>
> *2 Chronicles 24:18 And they left the house of the Lord God of their fathers, and served groves and idols: and wrath came upon Judah and Jerusalem for this their trespass.*

As you can see, God hates idols and apostasy. Also, apostasy is creating another idol in front of his face because now you are worshipping a false Jesus. You're worshipping something ELSE because you don't want to either comply with the restrictions of the God of Abraham, Isaac and Jacob, or your ignorant of the truth due to not searching this out yourself. The Bible says that ignorance is not acceptable. It can be no excuse on judgment day.

> *Hosea 4:6 - My people are destroyed for lack of knowledge: because thou hast rejected knowledge, I will also reject thee, that thou shalt be no priest to me: seeing thou hast forgotten the law of thy God, I will also forget thy children.*

 As you look at the list below of the idols, consider where we are at in Spring of 2020 in a global lockdown. Many of these idols have been stripped from us. Judgment has begun.

1. Whoredom
2. New Age & False Religions
3. Tattoos & Piercings
4. Ecumenical Movement & False UNITY
5. Emergent Church
6. Preacher Pyramid
7. Entertainment vs. Worship
8. Food & Gluttony
9. Technology & Social Media
10. Non-Prayer in our churches
11. Social Justice
12. Masons & Freemasons
13. Illuminati & Spirit of Antichrist
14. Greasy Grace & False Hope
15. Greed of Money in Ministry
16. Elitism & Cliques/Tribes
17. Time
18. Homosexuality & Sexual Perversion
19. Abortion
20. People Pleaser
21. Neglecting our families
22. Our Possessions/Material Things
23. Our own Image/Self
24. Witchcraft & Occult
25. Co-Dependence on the Government
26. Animal Worship
27. Traditions & Heritages
28. Pharmakeia & Drugs
29. Numbers & Statistics
30. Our Leaders/Celebrity Preachers
31. Programs & Itinerary
32. Human Intellect & Philosophy
33. Alcohol
34. Pornography & Sexual Perversion
35. Sports Worship
36. Politically Correct Society
37. Our Careers
38. Our Homes/Buildings or Location
39. Perfections & anti-disability
40. Our own ministry/business

The 40 Day Idols

If any of those idols hit your heart let's pray right now before we move any further that those are dealt with. Sometimes it is a daily fight. We must overcome daily. Let's pray:

Lord Jesus, please forgive me for this idol _____. I surrender this to you and I repent for placing it before you. Forgive me for not having self-control in this area. Please heal me and deliver me as I truly desire to please you in every area of my life. And Lord, my heart is to achieve my full destiny without these things holding me back. I do love you Lord more than I love any of these things. Please forgive me and I surrender my life to your will. In Jesus' name. Amen.

Although I'm warning that the New World Order is being setup 🖌️ 🖌️ etc...don't get me wrong. We are living in the most exciting times ever. 💯 💯 God called us for this. We knew we would be the generation to see the Antichrist. We knew that the Mark of the beast is coming etc. We knew a great falling away would happen etc.

The problem is that we was in it and just now opened our eyes.

Praise be to God! We are about to be used by God like never before! We will go through great persecution and what an honor that will be! Many of us will die for His name!

What an honor! We will see the 3rd temple and the Antichrist sitting there! We are the generation chosen for this! We will see so many miracles during the Great Tribulation and one day we will stand before God knowing we was the generation to be a part of this history!

Get ready Bride! We are about to walk in it! (if we are not already in it! I wonder sometimes)!!!

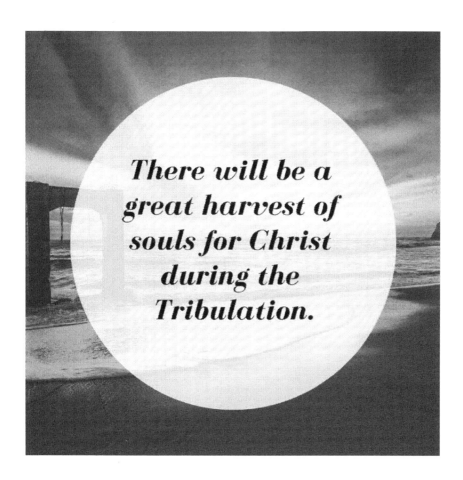

There will be a great harvest of souls for Christ during the Tribulation.

2
The Beast
We Face Now

Now that we know where we are at from the Apostasy and the Idols, what is the Beast we see now at the beginning of this judgment? He is a combination of three elements – like the trinity. The Lord gave me a visual of what we are facing and I want us to examine it.

What is the Beast?

As the one world order is coming together right before our eyes, the Lord has revealed to me what the Beast is. It is a merging of everything – government, economy, and religion. This is why the push for unity says that it brings prosperity and peace. We need to understand this so that we can prepare our families. We have very challenging days ahead and we must recognize our enemy head on.

The Beast is all corners wanting to flip from the OLD ORDER and switch to a NEW ORDER. They want to do away with individualism (each country, each state, each religion, each identity) and flip over to a universal identity. It is socialist in nature and wants everyone to conform to one image.

It is the Beast's image. They do not want anything to represent God's way of doing things. They want their Lucifer way of doing things.

NEW ORDER OF GOVERNMENT:

- No more countries having their own constitution or culture.
- No more laws separated by culture.
- One government that controls the masses.
- Everyone must share ALL – data, money, etc.
- There will be a set of guidelines for morals called the Noahide Laws in which the Orthodox Jews will control & Israel. The Jews will be the supreme race and the Gentiles are the ones that will be monitored with all these laws. We will have tribunals setup to make sure everyone abides by these laws. You can discover more at www.noahide.org. Anyone who does not abide by these laws will be beheaded. This also includes Christians who say that Jesus is the ONLY way to Heaven – even for Jews.

NEW ORDER OF MONEY/CURRENCY:
- No more separated money per country.
- No more cash where people can do things and not be monitored or traced.
- No more variances of dollar (one country higher or less)
- Everyone must have digital where it can all be traced and monitored.

- Everyone will have to have a chip inside of them so that they can be man-to-machine and can be connected to the grid – the Internet of Things.
- No more capitalism where you can change your whole identity and make more money than anyone else. Everyone must share and be divided out equally.
- There is coming a global RESET on the economic front

Notice how he talks in this presentation at the World Economic Forum about 5G's 4th Industrial Revolution. He speaks about 5G providing the technology for IoT, AI, etc. 5G is the juice/power to the Beast.

NEW ORDER OF RELIGION:

- Led by the New Apostolic Reformation, they desire to switch from the OLD ORDER of Christianity over to this new ecumenical universal Jesus. This new Christianity is now called KINGDOM so that it's more universally accepted. The term Christianity is too "rigid" and harsh with all the restrictions and boundaries in relation to sin. They are tired of the old preaching towards "sin-consciousness" and reasons people may go to Hell.
- On the left side of Christianity, it's a move towards Emergent Christianity in which they meet in a building and all sit on couches in a more relaxed atmosphere. The leader sits in the middle of the room and incorporates all religions. They may speak in tongues, participate in Catholic Mass, and perform a Labyrinth (a mystical New-Age style).
- They want to do away with all denominations, separate

factions of Protestant and Catholic, Seventh Day Adventists, Mormons, Islam, Hindu, Judaism, etc. No more individual separate views of their god. Now everyone serves the same god. Their god is tolerant of LGBTQ lifestyle, and label everything as universal love/tolerance.

- Ecumenical as far as drop the doctrinal differences and come together in agreement that they all serve A GOD. So, social justice is the mediator for all. Come together for the common good.

- No more vertical relationship between you as a person and God. They want to go towards a horizontal view of god. In the horizontal it's all about a universal Jesus, Christ-consciousness, common good, TOGETHER, As One, and you're locking arms in unity and not separated because of doctrine.

By merging together and calling the campaign TOGETHER. I believe it means:

To Get Her - ToGetHer

- It is a battle of the Beast to go to war with God and His Bride/Church. They hope to achieve this through technology. Through AI, they will be able to track all humans, create the global economy and fulfill Biblical prophecy.

This is a visual to what I'm trying to tell you is THE BEAST. THIS IS THE GREAT DECEPTION.

RELIGION + STATE + ECUMENISM = JUDGMENT BY GOD.

All of these three systems hope to flip.

Flip from OLD WAY OF GOVERNMENT TO NEW ONE WHERE WE'RE ALL ONE.

Flip from OLD CASH AND INDIVIDUAL COUNTRY'S MONEY SYSTEM TO NEW DIGITAL WHERE WE'RE ALL ONE.

Flip from OLD ORDER OF CHRISTIANITY AND RELIGION AND GO TO NEW APOSTOLIC ORDER (LIKE CATHOLICISM) AND MERGE WITH CATHOLICS AND ALL RELIGIONS AS ONE.

We're all TOGETHER (ToGetHer) now. Let's come together AS ONE.

THIS IS THE GREAT DECEPTION AND BEAST.

The triangle represents the order. The top we see the Q. Q is a psy-op in which he works at the White House and releases behind-the-scenes information all the time to keep the mystery going and pushing that Trump is our savior and he's fighting the Deep State. So, Q is always giving clues to the war going on with the evil Cabal within our government. The usual characters Q identifies are Nancy Pelosi, Hilary Clinton, Obama, etc. It paints the Democrats and evil people and the Republicans are the good people. He exposes evil actions in the government.

He always keeps people mesmerized with the mystical thoughts. I often wonder if Jonathan Cahn is not Q. His books have that same mystical language. Q has been used to bring everyone together as a common enemy of the Cabal/Deep State. This is how the LGBTQ community moved over to the Republican Party. This is how the religions are coming together as well. This and climate change. Everyone wants to get rid of evil sex-trafficking people, etc. So, let's all come together as one.

Then the economic is a switch from separate money to a unified money as cryptocurrency, etc. This is how they will merge with the chip so that it can all be connected. This will flip the economy from cash to digital currency.

The Beast will all work together to create a Golden Age and Utopia to remove God out of the equation. When you consider the UN's goals of Agenda 2030 and Bill Gate's Goal of chipping all humans in a vaccine, then we realize the Beast's goal to war against God and His creation. So, get ready Bride, the merging of all of this is THE BEAST SYSTEM.

This is the UN in New York City

The **UN is the Body** of the Beast, **IoT (AI) is the Brain** of the Beast, the **White House is the Mouth** of the Beast, **Capitol Hill is the Belly** of the Beast and **the Ecumenical Church is the Heart** of the Beast. **The Heart has cheated on God and tried to become its own god just like Lucifer did to God.** *He got prideful* and thought he was better. Same for the Beast on Earth now.

The Rockefeller Foundation conducted a scenario planning in which they mention a pandemic and how the world will come together to accept Beast control. Even in the Rockefeller Foundation scenario document called:

Scenarios for the Future of Technology
And International Development

At first, the **notion of a more controlled world gained wide acceptance and approval**. Citizens **willingly gave up** some of their sovereignty—**and their privacy**—to more paternalistic states in exchange for greater safety and stability. Citizens were more tolerant, and even eager, **for top-down direction and oversight, and national leaders had more latitude to impose order in the ways they saw fit.** In developed countries, this heightened oversight took many forms: **biometric IDs for all citizens**, for example, and tighter regulation of key industries whose stability was deemed vital to national interests. In many developed countries, enforced cooperation with a suite of new regulations and agreements slowly but steadily **restored both order and, importantly, economic growth.** (Knight, 2020)

It is well-known that the powers-that-be want to create **order out of chaos.** The Beast will create the perfect storm in order to control the masses. Look at the security we gave up on 9/11.

3

Biblical

End of Times

Knowing what the Bible says about the end of times in vital in this age of deception. I hope to bring some clarity to you. This is not an exhaustive book, but more of an overall view of the big picture for you to do more research. I will highlight main points for you to know. Jesus is coming back and if anyone tells you otherwise, you need to run!

BOOK OF REVELATION HIGHLIGHTS

I asked the Holy Spirit to teach me Revelation and one weekend I read it all the way through. I felt like God took me back in time to experience it. I will highlight some main key points! This is not an exhaustive study; just enough to prepare you for what's coming.

Rev 2:7 says that to him that overcomes will eat of the Tree of Life. Remember Bride that in the beginning with Adam and Eve we chose (mankind) the wrong tree. In the end, we will choose the right tree! It will cost us our life!

Rev 2:17 – Jesus is talking, and he talks about how he will give a white stone to those that eat of the hidden manna. In John 6 he explains to his disciples how he is the new manna that is a spiritual food. I love it that on this stone we will have a new name which no one will know except the one who receives it! Amazing!

The first few chapters Jesus is explaining how he feels about all the seven churches. Then in Chapter 4, John talks about God's throne. I noticed in verse 3 that there is a rainbow round about the throne. I feel that the homosexual agenda usingthe rainbow as their symbol is a smack in the face to God and his holiness. Terrible. This rainbow has six colors, which is lacking by one of the seven colors in God's rainbow. This reflects that LGBTQ colors are backwards. 666. God's seven is perfect reflection of completion. Also, this new cryptocurrency that's coming (the digital money), is called *Rainbow Currency*.

Then, before the throne is a sea of glass in verse 6. It says it is like unto crystal. This is key to later in the book.

Then the chapter talked about the four beasts that stand around the throne and say nothing all the time but, "Thou art worthy, O Lord, to receive glory and honor and power; for thou have created all things, and for thy pleasure they are and were created." How amazing is that! They constantly remind God how holy, beautiful and powerful!

Then in Chapter 5 we begin talking about all the seven seals. This is really touching when John cries and gets so upset because no one was worthy enough to open the book. Then, when Jesus stepped forth, I cried. How holy and beautiful is that? Jesus is the Lion of the Tribe of Judah, the root of David and was an overcomer! He was worthy!

o When he opened the book the 24 elders stood around him (12 apostles & 12 Children of Israel) and the four beasts! They had harps and golden vials filled with our prayers! Is this not amazing?

o Then they sang Jesus a song! Then angels sang!

In Chapter 6 we begin opening the seals. The different seals are different layers of judgment:

Seal One – *White Horse*. Man, on it had a bow and a crown was given to him. He went forth to conquer.

Seal Two – *Red Horse*. Power was given to him to take peace from the earth, and that they should kill one another. It was given unto him a great sword.

Seal Three – *Black Horse*. Had a pair of balances in his hand. Famine. A measure of wheat for a penny, and three measures of barley for a penny; and see that thou hurt not the oil and the wine.

Seal Four – *Pale Horse*. Death and Hell followed him. Power was given unto them over the ¼ part of the earth, to kill with sword, and with hunger (famine), and with death, and with the beasts of the earth. Sad.

Seal Five – *Martyrdom*. John saw under the altar the souls of them that were slain for the word of God and for the testimony which they held; and they cried out to God, "How Long O Lord, holy and true, dost thou not judge and avenge our blood on them that dwell on the earth? White robes were given unto every one of them. It was told to them to rest and hold on a little longer.

Seal Six – *The Rapture*. (This is my theory). At this point it talks about how the heaven rolls back like a scroll and Jesus appears and everyone is fearful and runs to the mountains. My theory is that it happens like this. When Jesus was dying on the cross and said, "It is finished", there was a great earthquake and all that. Well, same thing is happening right now.

So, now let's picture this. A great earthquake happens, and the sun became black as sackcloth of hair and the moon became as blood. Then the stars of heaven fell unto the earth, even as the fig tree casteth her untimely figs, when she is shaken of a mighty wind. Then the heaven departed as a scroll and every mountain and island were moved out of its place. I believe this signifies the time of the rapture. It says that the kings of the earth, the great men, the rich men, the chief captains and the mighty men, and every bondman, and every free man hid themselves in the dens and rocks of the mountains. They said to the mountains, "Fall on us and hide us from the face of him that sits on the throne, and from the wrath of the Lamb. For the great day of his wrath is come; and who shall be able to stand. I believe this is God separating the wheat from the tares. The tares know what is happening. Because the next verses in Chapter 7 talk about how they come and receive God's people before the wrath is poured out. It all happens at the same time. **THIS MUST MEAN THE RAPTURE IS MID-TRIB**. The first part of Tribulation (3.5 years), is meant as mercy to show people that they have one last chance to get saved before God's wrath is poured out!

Seal Six Cont'd in Chapter 7 – *Rapture and anointing of the 144,000 virgin Jew men of the tribes of Israel* to witness to people in the earth during the wrath. Four angels stand on the corners of the earth holding the four winds back so that wind will not blow on the earth, nor on the sea, nor on any tree (how sad that will be for the earth). An angel told the four angels not to hurt the earth or the sea until the 144,000 have been sealed by God on their foreheads. (Isn't it funny that during the wrath that God's people are sealed on their foreheads and so is Satan's people).

After they were all sealed, then rapture happens. The Bible says in 7:9 that a great multitude, which no man could number, of all nations, kindreds, people, and tongues stood before the throne, and before the Lamb, clothed with white robes and palms in their hands (how awesome is that!). They cried saying, "Salvation to our God which sitteth upon the throne, and unto the Lamb." Then all the angels stood round the throne, the elders and the four beasts and fell before the throne on their faces, and worshipped God. (How amazing that will be!).

Seal Seven – *Time was Still in Heaven for 30 Minutes*. **This is the transition to the wrath and heaven was so frozen in time due to the harshness that's about to be poured out.** Really this is showing the mercy of God to bring us home before all this happens. He has given mankind a chance to turn around for 3.5 years before this happened. Here they are loading up the seven angels with the seven trumpets, etc. I believe the seal was opening the wrath. See, one of the angels when the seal is opened brings all the censers of prayer and brings that smell before God. This is like reminding God of all the injustices and sadness of his people and what they had to endure on the Earth. Right after this, he goes into the temple and hides in his glory until this is all done. It's sad when you think about it. Right after God received the prayers, the angel took the censer and filled it with fire of the altar and cast it into the earth; and there were voices, and thundering and lightnings and an earthquake. Isn't that amazing Bride? Our prayers are literally letting the earth know that because of these, all this wrath is about to be poured out!

The First Trumpet – hail, fire mingled with blood and they were cast upon the earth and 1/3 part of the trees were burned up and all green grass was burned up!

The Second Trumpet – Mountain burning with fire into the sea – 1/3 sea became blood, 1/3 sea creatures died, and 1/3 part of the ships were destroyed.

The Third Trumpet – A great star (Wormwood) from heaven fell burning as a lamp. Fell on 1/3 part of the rivers and upon the fountains of the waters. 1/3 part of the waters became wormwood and many men died of the waters because they were made bitter.

The Fourth Trumpet – 1/3 part of the sun was smitten, and 1/3 part of the moon and 1/3 part of the stars so as the 1/3 part of them was darkened, the day shone not for a 1/3 part of it and the night likewise. At the same time an angel flew through the midst of the heaven saying with a loud voice, **"Woe, woe, woe, to the inhibiters of the earth by reason of the other voices of the trumpet of the three angels, which are yet to sound."** (Very sad! How much worse can it get?)

The Fifth Trumpet – (Chapter 9) – A star fell from heaven and it opened the pits of Hell and there arose a smoke out of the pit, as the smoke of a great furnace; and the sun and air were darkened by reason of the smoke of the pit. Out of the smoke came huge locusts and they were given power, as the scorpions of the earth have power.

- **Cannot hurt grass or any green thing, only Humans who do not have the mark of God on their forehead (the 144,000).** - It had commanded them that they should not kill them, but that they should be tormented five months; and their torment was as the torment of a scorpion, when he strikes a man. (How terrible! Ugh). The men will want to die but will not be able to!

- **The locusts were in the shapes of horses prepared until battle, and on their heads were as it were crowns like gold and faces like faces of men.** They have hair like women and teeth were as teeth of lions! They have breastplates as iron and the sound of their wings were as the sound of chariots of many horses running to battle. They have tails like scorpions and had stings in their tails. They have power to hurt man for five months.

- **They have a king over them called Apollyon.** This is the angel of the bottomless pit (isn't that crazy that there is an angel that oversees Hell?)

- **This fifth one ends the first woe** – two more to go.

The Sixth Trumpet – A voice sounded from the four horns of the golden altar, which is before God, saying "Loose the four angels which are bound in the great river Euphrates." The four were loosed, which were prepared for an hour, and a day, and a month, and a year to slay 1/3 part of men.

- **Number of horsemen were 200,000** – they have breastplates of fire, and of jacinth, and brimstone; and the heads of the horses were as the heads of lions; and out of their mouths issued fire and smoke and brimstone. (Kind of like they brought Hell up to the earth to torture mankind with it).

- **By these three were 1/3 part of men killed** – by fire, smoke and brimstone out of their mouths. (sounds like dragons)

- **Their power is in their mouth, and in their tails**; for their tails were like unto serpents, and had heads, and with them they do hurt.

31

- The other 2/3 of mankind still did not repent of the works of their hands, that they should not worship devils, and idols of gold, silver, and brass and stone, and of wood, **which** neither can see, nor hear or walk; neither repented they of their murders, nor of their sorceries, nor of their fornication, nor of their thefts.

The Seventh Trumpet - This is the most powerful one because it is not a plague, rather it's the announcement that time is done. It came from an angel clothed with a cloud and a rainbow was on his head. He had a little book in his hand and made John eat it! He sat his right foot on the sea and his left foot on the earth. This ended time!

There is so much more in the Book of Revelation. We have the two witnesses, the Antichrist, the seven bowls, etc. However, it would take too long to examine all those.

FALSE PROPHETS EVERYWHERE

This must be addressed because Jesus spent more time warning about this so that people may be aware that this will be rampant in the last days. I took many notes about this subject in the Bible:

Out Of 2 Peter:
- Bring damnable heresies
- Deny the Lord bought them
- Bring upon themselves swift destruction
- Many shall follow their pernicious ways; by reason of whom the way of truth shall be evil spoken of!
- This means they will talk evil of people speaking TRUTH!

- Through covetousness shall they with feigned words make merchandise of you
- In other words, they will lie to you and sell you a bunch of garbage for the money. I see ministers doing this all the time. They make up things for prophets. They come up with "ox anointings and owl anointings" etc. "Jezebel this and Jezebel that", write a book about it and people just buy it like crazy. They sell this mess to the masses.
- They will face judgment and damnation

Chapter 1:4-8 talks about the various judgments of God and how he will get vengeance in the end. (Noah, Lot, angels, etc.)

- God knows how to take care of his own
- He reserves the unjust for judgment day
- Chiefly those that walk after the flesh in the lust of uncleanness & despise government.
- Presumptuous are they; they are not afraid to speak evil of dignitaries.
- Whereas angels, which are great in power and might, bring not railing accusation against them before the Lord
- But these as natural brute beasts, made to be taken and destroyed speak evil of the things they understand not and shall utterly perish in their own corruption.
- He that speaketh of himself seeketh his own glory, but he that seeketh his glory that sent him; the same is true and no unrighteous is in him. (John 7:18)
- If ye continue in my word, then you are my disciples (John 8:31)

In 2 Chronicles 22-26 it talks about false prophets being a judgment to the church. Swelling words is a curse to any people. Truth must reign.

MARK OF THE BEAST

I talk about this in my previous book titled *Mark of the Beast*. I also address this in my next book, *The Last American Bride*. Basically, they are going to require each human to be implanted with the RFID (Radio Frequency Identification Device) either in their hands or their foreheads. It may also be released in a gel combined with computer chips or an immunization shot/vaccine which would have chips that connect you to the Beast. We will know if it is the mark by them requiring you to be a part of their system by doing???? So, if they tell you that you will not be able to buy or sell by participating in this action then you know.

For instance, we are in a global lockdown now (Spring 2020) and there is speculation that they will not let us back into society unless we get a vaccine, chip, gel or shot to where they can "surveillance" society. They need to monitor who has a fever, symptoms, etc., in order to trust us back in society. So, if they tell us that we cannot participate in life in this world unless we do things their way to be marked and tagged like cattle then we know we cannot do that. We are the temple of God.

ANTICHRIST
(False Christ or New Age Christ)

The Antichrist is the false messiah. After all my research I have learned so much about this coming "Christ" that is so shocking! For one thing, he will claim to be the real Messiah!

He will claim that he is god and will be the universal Christ that everyone (New Age and the one world religion) anticipated. He is waiting for the Earth to be in oneness and UNITY before he steps on the scene. Chapter 15 in Revelation talks about him:

- He will be granted power and authority
- One of his heads was wounded to death but comes back to life
- Mankind will worship him thinking no one can touch him
- He spoke great blasphemies and did that for 3.5 years
- Makes war with the saints and kills them
- He was given power over all nations, tribes and tongues
- Everyone worships him except the remnant!

Then Great Beast comes on the scene:

- Has two horns like a lamb and speaks as a dragon
- Causes everyone to worship the first beast
- Does great wonders (fire from heaven)
- Deceives the Earth by the means of those miracles and causes them to make an image to the beast
- He gave power to give life to the beast, so it spoke and
- caused those that didn't worship the image to be killed
- Caused all to be marked in right hand or forehead so that no man may buy or sell unless marked
- His number is 666
- He will cause a war in the earth against Jesus and his army. This is the Battle of Armageddon
- He loses and is bound for 1,000 years, then to be loosed for a short season. (time is not known)
- He shall speak great words against the highest and shall

wear out the saints of the highest and think to change times and laws; and they shall be given into his hand for 3.5 years.

Daniel 8: 24-25 - 24 And his power shall be mighty, but not by his own power: and he shall destroy wonderfully, and shall prosper, and practise, and shall destroy the mighty and the holy people. 25 And through his policy also he shall cause craft to prosper in his hand; and he shall magnify himself in his heart, and by peace shall destroy many: he shall also stand up against the Prince of princes; but he shall be broken without hand.

ISRAEL & PEACE PLANS

We will know that time officially starts for the Tribulation whenever there is a seven (7) year peace treaty signed between Israel and Palestine. The key will be if Jerusalem gives up some land to the Palestinians. Once this peace accord is signed then the seven years begins.

President Trump and his son-in-law completed the Trump Peace Plan. However, at this point they have not agreed and signed it. I believe it's a prelude to the Antichrist fulfilling it.

Zechariah 12:2-3 - 2 Behold, I will make Jerusalem a cup of trembling unto all the people round about, when they shall be in the siege both against Judah and against Jerusalem. And in that day will I make Jerusalem a burdensome stone for all people: all that burden themselves with it shall be cut in pieces, though all the people of the earth be gathered together against it.

When it is complete, be ready for whatever country participated in that deal and helped to split Jerusalem, God's holy city, then it is prophesied that God will literally split America in half at the Mississippi River. Either way, this deal is soon to happen because God wrote about it in the Book of Daniel.

> *Daniel 9:27 And he shall confirm the covenant with many for one week: and in the midst of the week he shall cause the sacrifice and the oblation to cease, and for the overspreading of abominations he shall make it desolate, even until the consummation, and that determined shall be poured upon the desolate.*

However, I must tell you Bride that I interviewed Steve DeNoon of Israeli News LIVE and he said that he does not believe they will tell us when they officially sign that Peace Deal. I do not believe they will either and when President Trump officially finished that plan in January 2020, he did an official ceremony in the White House. Why would he do that if it wasn't official? He likes to win!

SEVEN YEAR TRIBULATION

Following the Peace Plan, the seven (7) years officially begin. Then we have the first 3.5 years which is the mercy of God in judgment. It is the opening of the seals and famine, pestilence and sword. The first 3.5 years is great persecution to the Christians and death. It is the implementation of the mark of the beast (chip).

The temple is also built during the first 3.5.

I saw a prophecy where they said it may be a virtual reality temple in which people can use the glasses to experience it. Also, this may be a way for the Beast to promote receiving the chip between the eyes (close to the 3rd eye – New Age).

The ones who receive it there will be able to see extra things like that. It makes sense though with the roll-out of 5G internet for the Internet of Things. I talk more about the technology coming in the next book.

The rapture happens mid-trib when it talks about heaven stopping for 30 minutes. This is when the angel assigns the 144,000 out of the 12 Tribes of Israel. Then:

> *Revelation 7:9-17 - 9 After this I beheld, and, lo, a great multitude, which no man could number, of all nations, and kindreds, and people, and tongues, stood before the throne, and before the Lamb, clothed with white robes, and palms in their hands; 10 And cried with a loud voice, saying, Salvation to our God which sitteth upon the throne, and unto the Lamb. 11 And all the angels stood round about the throne, and about the elders and the four beasts, and fell before the throne on their faces, and worshipped God, 12 Saying, Amen: Blessing, and glory, and wisdom, and thanksgiving, and honour, and power, and might, be unto our God for ever and ever. Amen. 13 And one of the elders answered, saying unto me, What are these which are arrayed in white robes? and whence came they? 14 And I said unto him, Sir, thou knowest. And he said to me, These are they which came out of great tribulation, and have washed their robes, and made them white in the blood of the Lamb. 15 Therefore are they before the throne of God, and serve him day and night in his temple: and he that sitteth on the throne shall dwell among them. 16 They shall hunger no more, neither thirst anymore; neither shall the sun light on them, nor*

any heat. 17 For the Lamb which is in the midst of
the throne shall feed them, and shall lead them
unto living fountains of waters: and God shall wipe
away all tears from their eyes.

Then, this is the second woe (part of the second 3.5 years of wrath), the two witnesses step on the scene. Some say they are Moses and Elijah. It is kind of confusing as to when these two men step on the scene, but whether it's the first part or second is irrelevant if we know it's during the seven-year period. These two are warning mankind that time is over, and they need to repent. Either way, these two men are here as two very visible warnings to mankind.

They will have the power to pour out any type of pestilence, famine by shutting up the heavens, etc. No one can kill them. Doesn't this sound impossible given today's technology! They can't bomb them, nuke them, shoot them, blow them up or nothing! Powerful!

Revelation 11:3-19 - 3 And I will give power unto
my two witnesses, and they shall prophesy a
thousand two hundred and threescore days,
clothed in sackcloth. 4 These are the two olive trees,
and the two candlesticks standing before the God
of the earth. 5 And if any man will hurt them, fire
proceedeth out of their mouth, and devoureth their
enemies: and if any man will hurt them, he must in
this manner be killed. 6 These have power to shut
heaven, that it rain not in the days of their
prophecy: and have power over waters to turn
them to blood, and to smite the earth with all
plagues, as often as they will.

7 And when they shall have finished their testimony, the beast that ascendeth out of the bottomless pit shall make war against them, and shall overcome them, and kill them. 8 And their dead bodies shall lie in the street of the great city, which spiritually is called Sodom and Egypt, where also our Lord was crucified. 9 And they of the people and kindreds and tongues and nations shall see their dead bodies three days and an half, and shall not suffer their dead bodies to be put in graves. 10 And they that dwell upon the earth shall rejoice over them, and make merry, and shall send gifts one to another; because these two prophets tormented them that dwelt on the earth. 11 And after three days and an half the spirit of life from God entered into them, and they stood upon their feet; and great fear fell upon them which saw them. 12 And they heard a great voice from heaven saying unto them, Come up hither. And they ascended up to heaven in a cloud; and their enemies beheld them. 13 And the same hour was there a great earthquake, and the tenth part of the city fell, and in the earthquake were slain of men seven thousand: and the remnant were affrighted, and gave glory to the God of heaven.

They are clothed in sackcloth. This is how they grieved in the Bible. I take this as they are grieving for mankind!

Then, it's also sad how people were rejoicing when they were killed.

Those men brought them so much misery that they were glad to get rid of them! Can you believe Bride that they don't know in the word that these men will just rise from the dead in 3 ½ days? They probably will not know because by this time they will have confiscated the bibles, shut off all conservative and Christian voices online, and the Christians are gone, so they have no more good on the earth. It's all wrath and evil being poured out. So much so, that God hid himself while all this is happening. Sad.

There are some scholars who believe that it's not actually two men but time periods and cities. I believe it is literally men.

CITIES OF REFUGE

There will be places for Christians to go during Tribulation for refuge and healing. American Family Association describes these in the Bible as, "Cities of refuge were places where someone who had committed involuntary manslaughter could flee and find safety until the day of his trial." (AFA, 2017). These were cities of protection to God's people. During Tribulation there will be cities all over America as well.

> *Joshua 20:3 - That the slayer that killeth any person unawares and unwittingly may flee thither: and they shall be your refuge from the avenger of blood.*

In Deuteronomy it talks about six cities of refuge. I thought it was ironic that God marked six cities for me on the *MAGA Revival Tour* in 2017. There were six cities that he required me to prophesy over those cities.

The Lord instructed that there would be six cities across US. Three on the East side of the Mississippi and three on the West.

East

Miami, FL – prayed at the Port in Miami

Niagara Falls NY – prayed at the falls and prophesied in both

Canada side and US side

Pawtucket, RI – prayed at a native-American historical place by river

West

New Orleans, LA – prayed at a port

El Paso, TX – prayed at the border crossing into Mexico

Jamestown, ND – prayed at their courthouse

The prophecies are long, so I won't give them all (I may put them in another book where I write more detail about the tour). Here is a couple:

Niagara Falls, NY

- Declare that that the cleansing waters from the throne is coming to the church and expose the sins and iniquities in the leadership.
- Corruption will be exposed.
- Judgment is coming to the House of the Lord. It will reveal the muddy waters from the throne from one end of the nation to the other.
- A great fear of the Lord is coming to the Church.
- God wants his Bride without spot and wrinkle.
- The crystal-clear waters from the throne will purify the church like a mighty rushing wind. It will become muddy waters as it flows off the cliff as a mighty rushing waves is how the judgment will come to the church.
- Pray for revival of purity and holiness coming from the throne of God.

- Remove the world out of the church who has been tainted the alters with the world.

- As the mighty waters flow over this nation, it will flow over the hard clay and dirt and residue from the past and the hard shells will all be cleaned off to expose the beautiful jewels and diamonds that God needs to reveal to the Earth.

- This cleansing will be of great magnitude. From the mega to the minor will be exposed so truth will reign in the nation.

- Lord, I pray that the ministers will repent and heed the warning. Ministers will get their life right, so they will not hurt the Body of Christ.

- Heal your leaders Lord. Heal the false and reveal the true.

- Expose the leaders operating in corruption in the government. Heal our government from the president down.

- A great exposure of the fake and false will be revealed as the truth is exalted and elevated.

- I'm calling in the cleansing clear waters from the throne to flood this nation from one end to the other to expose every corruption and false idol.

- I dispatch angels to open the gates to the throne and the waters to pour over the nation for money and other.

- I pray against sexual perversion in the nation.

- I pray against mixing the world in the church, tainting the alters of purity.

- The injustices of the past and the blood that is crying out to God would be healed.

- I prayed on the American side of the falls and on the Canada side.

43

Pawtucket Rhode Island

- Pray for the healing of the nations
- Forgiveness of the races and Unity of the land
- Pray for Native Americans and African Americans healing
- I prayed this beside a beautiful flowing river

Jamestown, North Dakota

- He said to go to the courthouse and pray
- He said to pray for healing in the land there
- Restoration of covenant that he made with Jamestown
- Pray against corruption in government in for the evil to be exposed and righteousness to prevail in the city
- Pray for the Hidden jewels to begin to be revealed
- Pray for healing of the nations there and healing of the tribes of the Native American Indians
- Play for ancient ancestral curses to be broken over the stadium for the prophetic activation to be released over the city

I prayed over the following cities, but they were not part of the original six:

Portland Maine

I am to go to Portland Maine and go to the beach the ocean the border and pray over the ocean and the border for the eastern side of the United States pray to secure the border.

"Go through, go through the gates; prepare ye the way of the people; cast up, cast up the highway; gather out the stones; lift up a standard for the people. Behold, the Lord hath proclaimed unto the end of the world, Say ye to the daughter of Zion, Behold, thy salvation cometh; behold, his reward is with him, and his work before him. And they shall call them, The holy people, The redeemed of the Lord: and thou shalt be called, Sought out, A city not forsaken." Isaiah 62:10-12 KJV

Claremont New Hampshire

The Lord told me to go to the courthouse and pray for justice to rain in our nation. Truth and justice pray against corruption in our lives as well.

NOTES ABOUT REFUGE CITIES

I prayed across the entire border of the United States. I also prayed at the border of Canada and the State of Washington.

Also, there was a huge homosexual demon in the State of Maine in the northeast towns and I prayed against it. I also came against a strong death demon and high occult in Newark Pennsylvania.

So, when things get rough in the country, ask the Lord to show you where those cities are.

You may be near one. You will need to know where these are because they will have a supernatural dome over them. The Lord showed me this in the spirit. The children of God will be protected there for a while. In these places you will have food and provision and a community to partner with. It's much better to be with help.

NEW WORLD ORDER

This is when the world comes together under one government and partners with the one world religion so that the Antichrist can step on the scene and fulfill the end of times. This New World Order is proceeded by the New Age Peace Plan. This is to bring peace to the world and have a big Utopia on the earth with the new Christ on the scene who will take all the other gods and form one big blissful earth. This is what they will call the Aquarian Age (Golden Age).

This New World Order is led by the United Nations and all ran by the Jesuits, Catholic Church, Illuminati, etc.

Look at this graph:

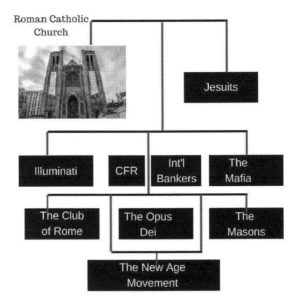

See how the New Age Movement is the root of it! It is! This New World Order will enforce the mark, laws, & worldly government.

Wedding of Prince Andrew & Meghan Markle

When I watched this wedding, there were things I noticed that I want to include in my book just in case something comes out of it later. The wedding was Illuminati all the way around. First, it's a setup for a prince in the UK to marry a divorced woman, mixed, parents divorced, etc. However, at the wedding the commentators made the remark that the monarchy wanted to give impressions of having a diverse throne. Meghan had many black friends there, a black preacher (who preached ecumenical to the core and sounded like he prepared the way for the false), etc

At the wedding, she had her mother with her, but her father did not come. They said on one program that he was embarrassed and didn't want to make her look bad. I felt sorry for him. He ended up not walking her down the aisle. Prince Charles did.

Then the floor in the room where she got married was black and white checkers. Then her crown (which the Queen loaned to her for the wedding and it was from Queen Mary!), had an all-seeing eye in the middle of it. Meghan also didn't have brides' maids. It was very strange. Here are pictures I took:

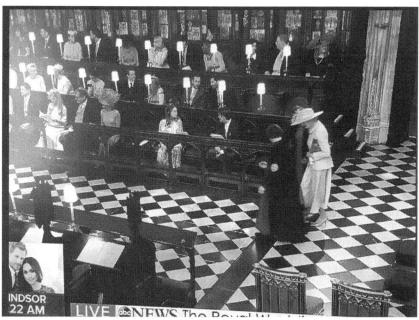

49

They bragged about Meghan being a **feminist and really into social justice.** These are key words to the one world religion as well! Keep your eyes open concerning this prince.

- The Illuminati connections:
- We must consider all the Illuminati entertainment leaders were there such as Oprah, George Clooney, and a bunch of other actors.
- Meghan invited the preacher who preached this New Age Jesus.
- Married in a Catholic Church.
- Black and White Checked Floor
- All-seeing eye on her crown
- United States and England marrying as a unity gesture as well.

Excerpts from Michael Bruce Curry –
27th Presiding Bishop and Primate – Episcopal Church:

We must discover the power of love. Once we do that, we can make of this old world a new one. There's power in love. When you love, and you show it, it just feels right.

There's a reason for it. We were made by a power of love. Our loves are meant to be in that love. Therefore, we are here. The source of love is God himself. (sounds good so far huh?). **Insert note – If you can watch his sermon you need to. I am cracking up at the Queen and the royal's reactions to the African American fired up preacher! Ha ha!**

Imagine a world where love is the way. Our homes, neighborhoods and communities where love is the way. Imagine where nations and business and commerce are the way. Unselfish, sacrificial, and redemptive then no child will go to bed hungry. When love is the way poverty will be history and the earth will be our sanctuary.

When love is he way there's plenty of good room for God's children. When love is the way we treat each other like we're family. When love is the way we know that God is the source of us all, and we are brothers and sisters and children of God.

That's a new heaven and a new earth. A new world. A new human family. Ole Solomon was right in the Old testament – that is fire. He then recites from Pierre Teilhard de Chardin SJ; a Jesuit, Roman-Catholic Priest, mystic and scientist, "The discovery or invention or harnessing of fire was one of great scientific and technological discoveries in all of human history."

Fire made human civilization possible. Fire is what brings about real change like the industrial revolution. Fire is what brings us this technology. De Chardin said that if humanity ever harnesses that fire again; if humanity ever captures that energy of love, it will be the second time in history that we have discovered fire." Dr. King was right, we must discover that power of love. When we do, we will make of this old world a new world. My brother and my sister, God love you and God bless you and may God hold us all in those almighty hands of love.

My Thoughts

The reason I said New Age Christ is because of what he said in the end. What is this FIRE that created technology and changed orders and worlds? Only in Satan's kingdom. This terminology of going out of the old order into the new and everyone coming together is the New World Order, one world religion, New Apostolic Reformation language. They are all speaking of turning from the traditional way of life to this New Age Utopia.

Now this couple has stepped out of the throne and royalty to travel the world? How did they get out of their duties so easily? It is very suspicious. For what? **Is it to prepare and partner with the Antichrist?** I believe we haven't seen the end of those two.

ONE WORLD RELIGION

The One world religion is led by the Catholic Church. Rome is at the root of this one. It is at the root, but they partner with the Noahide Laws. The State Department started a new division called International Religious Freedom. One of their programs is "Abrahamic Initiative" in which all three main religions come together. I believe this is the merging of faiths with Catholicism at the root. Look at this graph that the Lord gave me:

This shows you how they are all related. I'm not going to focus on this too much now because it's all in these three books. However, the one world religion is working to pull all the religions together to form one religion and this will basically turn on the original Christians. They will kill us. They are also setting the stage for the Antichrist and the beast system.

Israel & Jerusalem Update

This is Jerod Kushner at the 70th Anniversary of Israel Celebration. It is also a dedication of the United States Embassy moving to Jerusalem. It is a miracle that the United States recognized Jerusalem as Israel's capital! However, as great as this is, I want you to notice the writing. It said ALL FAITHS TOGETHER. This is key because one day they are going to make Jerusalem the capital of all religions! This will be the ecumenical capital! This whole event was setting up for the New World Order.

After he finished this agenda, now he is over the supply chain for the Coronavirus Task Force with FEMA.

Here's more pictures:

The above is the Ambassador to Israel.

Above is Benjamin Netanyahu – Prime Minister of Israel

The Above is President Trump's Daughter & Son-in-Law. It's because of Jerod Kushner's hard work that this all happened in Israel.

Pastor John Hagee delivered the ending prayer at the celebration. Now I understand that he's a big part of this apostasy because his CUFI organization does not focus on winning the Jews to Jesus. It focuses on winning Christians to Israel cause. This brings billions of dollars to Israel to fund the Noahide Laws. If his organization was legit, then Israel would not partner with him because they do not want to convert to Christianity. They want to turn Gentiles towards them.

IRAN AND NEW WORLD ORDER

I discovered on Twitter a trending subject and was shocked! I know God brought to my attention before these books are released. It's about the communist group/socialists who are working to overthrow the Iran regime. Guess who was there to help in this cause? Rudy Giuliani! The president's lawyer!

He gave the lady leader a signed document from America showing their support for their agenda to overturn the regime in Iran!

It rests on pluralism, separation of religion and state

Maryam Rajavi

She also has the Pope's support, she almost has the UN's support, and has Europe's support. In other words, the NWO is on her side. What she says is telling of the New Age agenda!

MARTYRDOM

I address this in more detail in the next book as well. However, I do want to point out that during Tribulation, Christians will be killed. So, martyrdom is coming in America on a level we've never seen. People have been killed all over the world for Jesus' name, but we haven't seen the level that they have. We are about to! As I'm showing you what's happening globally in Jerusalem and Iran, the New World Order is pushing through at an unprecedented rate. More on this in *The Last American Bride* book.

RAPTURE & SECOND COMING

After my studies in the scriptures, I have concluded that the rapture is mid-tribulation (after the first 3.5 years) because Matthew 24 and Luke and all other scriptures do not backup a pre-trib rapture. We will have to go through suffering. My point on all of that is why not church? Why not to gain more souls? Why do we want to be selfish and leave? We need to be on the earth if God will allow so that we may win souls for his kingdom (I mean the real kingdom too!). So, we will go through the first 3.5 years. I have friends who believe in pre-trib and others who believe in post-trib. As long as we KNOW that He IS coming back!

Revelation 14:13-16 - 13 And I heard a voice from heaven saying unto me, Write, Blessed are the dead which die in the Lord from henceforth: Yea, saith the Spirit, that they may rest from their labours; and their works do follow them. 14 And I looked, and behold a white cloud, and upon the cloud one sat like unto the Son of man, having on his head a golden crown, and in his hand a sharp sickle. 15 And another angel came out of the temple, crying with a loud voice to him that sat on the cloud, Thrust in thy sickle, and reap: for the time is come for thee to reap; for the harvest of the earth is ripe. 16 And he that sat on the cloud thrust in his sickle on the earth; and the earth was reaped.

Then Jesus will come midway through and take us home before the angel swings the sickle for the sin harvest. This is so sad!

Revelation 14:17-20 - 17 And another angel came out of the temple which is in heaven, he also having a sharp sickle. 18 And another angel came out from the altar, which had power over fire; and cried with a loud cry to him that had the sharp sickle, saying, Thrust in thy sharp sickle, and gather the clusters of the vin e of the earth; for her grapes are fully ripe. 19 And the angel thrust in his sickle into the earth, and gathered the vine of the earth, and cast it into the great winepress of the wrath of God. 20 And the winepress was trodden without the city, and blood came out of the winepress, even unto the horse bridles, by the space of a thousand and six hundred furlongs.

This officially kicks off the remaining 3.5 years of wrath. The Christians are gone, and the wrath is so terrible that time stopped in heaven for 30 minutes before the angel was released!

Then, at the end of the seven (7) years tribulation is the second coming. Jesus comes back on his white horse with the army to do war with the beast.

> ***Revelation 17:12-14 - 12 And the ten horns which thou sawest are ten kings, which have received no kingdom as yet; but receive power as kings one hour with the beast. 13 These have one mind, and shall give their power and strength unto the beast. 14 These shall make war with the Lamb, and the Lamb shall overcome them: for he is Lord of lords, and King of kings: and they that are with him are called, and chosen, and faithful.***

The Christians that were raptured up mid-trib are at the marriage supper of the lamb:

> ***Revelation 19:5-10 - 5 And a voice came out of the throne, saying, Praise our God, all ye his servants, and ye that fear him, both small and great. 6 And I heard as it were the voice of a great multitude, and as the voice of many waters, and as the voice of mighty thunderings, saying, Alleluia: for the Lord God omnipotent reigneth. 7 Let us be glad and rejoice, and give honour to him: for the marriage of the Lamb is come, and his wife hath made herself ready. 8 And to her was granted that she should be arrayed in fine linen, clean and white: for the fine linen is the righteousness of saints.***

9 And he saith unto me, Write, Blessed are they which are called unto the marriage supper of the Lamb. And he saith unto me, These are the true sayings of God. 10 And I fell at his feet to worship him. And he said unto me, See thou do it not: I am thy fellowservant, and of thy brethren that have the testimony of Jesus: worship God: for the testimony of Jesus is the spirit of prophecy.

Then comes Jesus on his white horse to officially end time and take care of the beast:

Revelation 19: 11-21 - 11 And I saw heaven opened, and behold a white horse; and he that sat upon him was called Faithful and True, and in righteousness he doth judge and make war. 12 His eyes were as a flame of fire, and on his head were many crowns; and he had a name written, that no man knew, but he himself.

13 And he was clothed with a vesture dipped in blood: and his name is called The Word of God. 14 And the armies which were in heaven followed him upon white horses, clothed in fine linen, white and clean. 15 And out of his mouth goeth a sharp sword, that with it he should smite the nations: and he shall rule them with a rod of iron: and he treadeth the winepress of the fierceness and wrath of Almighty God. 16 And he hath on his vesture and on his thigh a name written, King Of Kings, And Lord Of Lords.

17 And I saw an angel standing in the sun; and he cried with a loud voice, saying to all the fowls that fly in the midst of heaven, Come and gather yourselves together unto the supper of the great God; 18 That ye may eat the flesh of kings, and the flesh of captains, and the flesh of mighty men, and the flesh of horses, and of them that sit on them, and the flesh of all men, both free and bond, both small and great. 19 And I saw the beast, and the kings of the earth, and their armies, gathered together to make war against him that sat on the horse, and against his army. 20 And the beast was taken, and with him the false prophet that wrought miracles before him, with which he deceived them that had received the mark of the beast, and them that worshipped his image. These both were cast alive into a lake of fire burning with brimstone. 21 And the remnant were slain with the sword of him that sat upon the horse, which sword proceeded out of his mouth: and all the fowls were filled with their flesh.

As you probably noticed Bride, when he comes in the rapture, he is taking us UP to him for the Marriage Supper of the Lamb.

When he comes in the second coming, he is not taking Christians up. He is coming in the clouds to bring war to the Beast and his followers WITH the saints. We are coming back!

MILLENNIAL REIGN

Scripture says it all:

> *Revelation 20:4-6 - 4 And I saw thrones, and they sat upon them, and judgment was given unto them: and I saw the souls of them that were beheaded for the witness of Jesus, and for the word of God, and which had not worshipped the beast, neither his image, neither had received his mark upon their foreheads, or in their hands; and they lived and reigned with Christ a thousand years. 5 But the rest of the dead lived not again until the thousand years were finished. This is the first resurrection. 6 Blessed and holy is he that hath part in the first resurrection: on such the second death hath no power, but they shall be priests of God and of Christ, and shall reign with him a thousand years.*

As you can tell, the ones that make it THROUGH tribulation and do not take the mark are able to live with Jesus during the 1,000-year reign (Millennial Reign). We shall be priests of God!

Then Satan will be loosed for a time and he shall go out to deceive the nations which are in the four corners of the earth. Gog and Magog, to gather them together to battle. Apparently, the devil goes around the earth and tries to deceive them again to come battle Jesus and the people in the city. However, God stops them and "fire came down from God out of heaven, and devoured them." (Rev 20:9).

If you will partner with the beast now while the
day is prosperous
and the sun shining,
for your gain of open doors,
speaking engagements, networks, and ungodly
associations; then you will take The mark of the
beast when the pressure is on and
survival depends on it.
If you cannot stand up for God
now you won't later.

Compromise now for a little
bowl of porridge
or stand up to the
beast for the robe later

#SAYNOTOECUMENICALMOVEMENT

Revelation 20:10 And the devil that deceived them was cast into the lake of fire and brimstone, where the beast and the false prophet are, and shall be tormented day and night for ever and ever.

Following this event is the Great White Throne Judgment. We must know that our names are written in the Lamb's Book of Life!

NOTES ABOUT END OF TIMES

Just remember Bride that we do not fear all these things. God has created us for such a time as this. These books are here to prepare you for it. It is to open your eyes, equip you and to cause you to make wise decisions in the future so that we can reap the most harvest!

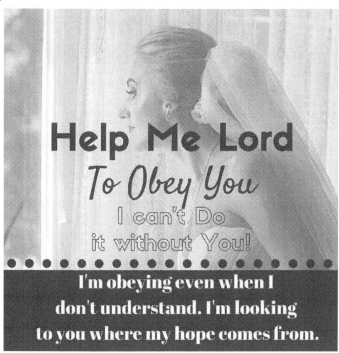

Isn't it amazing that God chose you to live right now? He knew all this was coming and put you here. It is for a reason! Pray today and ask God how he can use you in the rest of time here.

By America partnering with the Beast and passing laws by the liberals, leftists, socialists, communists, etc., it opens the door for God's judgment. We did it to ourselves.

DR. JUNE KNIGHT

**SAY NO!
TO THE
COMPROMISING
CHURCH!**

4

Clash of Two Kingdoms

We are in the middle of an epic showdown right now in the Body of Christ. Do we believe most of the church which is ecumenical now? This group consists of the Emergent Church and the NAR – New Apostolic Reformation people. They are the Kingdom Now people who call everything Kingdom of God. They say they are bringing the Kingdom of God from Heaven down to Earth, and many of the ministers in this movement do not even know what they're involved in.

These are coming together in mass unity in partnership with the great whore of Babylon – the Mother Church (she likes to say) – The Catholic Church. I will get in more detail later about the characteristics of this group and what to look for and how to identify them.

> *Ephesians 5:1-12 - 1 Be ye therefore followers of God, as dear children; 2 And walk in love, as Christ also hath loved us, and hath given himself for us an offering and a sacrifice to God for a sweet smelling savour.*

3 But fornication, and all uncleanness, or covetousness, let it not be once named among you, as becometh saints; 4 Neither filthiness, nor foolish talking, nor jesting, which are not convenient: but rather giving of thanks. 5 For this ye know, that no whoremonger, nor unclean person, nor covetous man, who is an idolater, hath any inheritance in the kingdom of Christ and of God. 6 Let no man deceive you with vain words: for because of these things cometh the wrath of God upon the children of disobedience. 7 Be not ye therefore partakers with them. 8 For ye were sometimes darkness, but now are ye light in the Lord: walk as children of light: 9 (For the fruit of the Spirit is in all goodness and righteousness and truth;) 10 Proving what is acceptable unto the Lord. 11 And have no fellowship with the unfruitful works of darkness, but rather reprove them. 12 For it is a shame even to speak of those things which are done of them in secret. 13 But all things that are reproved are made manifest by the light: for whatsoever doth make manifest is light. 14 Wherefore he saith, Awake thou that sleepest, and arise from the dead, and Christ shall give thee light. 15 See then that ye walk circumspectly, not as fools, but as wise, 16 Redeeming the time, because the days are evil. 17 Wherefore be ye not unwise, but understanding what the will of the Lord is. 18 And be not drunk with wine, wherein is excess; but be filled with the Spirit; 19 Speaking to yourselves in psalms and hymns and spiritual songs, singing and making melody in your heart to the Lord;

> **20 Giving thanks always for all things unto God and the Father in the name of our Lord Jesus Christ; 21 Submitting yourselves one to another in the fear of God.**

As you can tell by the previous scripture, God wants us to depart from sin and the appearance of evil. He hates mixing.

He does not like us bringing untruths into the gospel. If so, it is no longer the gospel. This is how they are convincing people of this dangerous narrative is that they are producing 95% truth. Maybe even 80%. Most people are not studiers of the word of God and may not know how to test the spirits against the word of God. I pray that you are. I pray that you weigh all things said in this book carefully, do your research, and pray about it. Never believe any person as they know it all or are God himself! Trust only the word of God and the Holy Ghost. The Holy Ghost works in unison with the word of God. They are not apart from each other.

We are at a crossroads in our country. Do we believe the narrative of the majority flow and listen to their interpretation of what's coming, or do we follow the gloom and doom preachers who say judgment is coming, repent, and get ready to die for His name, etc.? One road says peace and other road says trouble ahead. We must examine these two paths because my interpretation is that we are back in the garden choosing between which tree to eat.

The Tree of Knowledge of Good and Evil

The Tree of Knowledge of Good and Evil represents the Kingdom Now movement because they are seeking after signs miracles and wonders and all the extra-biblical knowledge to be more of a superpower on the Earth.

You will learn that they want more control in their arms of flesh (Tree of Knowledge of Good and Evil represents arm of flesh). They are wanting to build up this kingdom on Earth – but only one available is Antichrist.

We will examine the fruits of this with such beliefs as the Courts of Heaven, Seven Mountain Mandate, contemplative prayer, astral-projection, grave-sucking, destiny (tarot) cards, etc.

It's focusing so much on the experience and knowing everything that it leaves out faith. Bill Johnson expresses this as, "He's wanting to raise up a generation of people who will want to learn to live from the presence of God as opposed to living merely from the principles of God. And that's a big deal because in the principles there is success, but from the presence there is no failure". (Johnson, A Mess- Heidi Baker - Bill Johnson - Rolland Baker - Bethel Redding, 2017) This belief once again stresses experience over truth. This is very dangerous. Principles represent the ten commandments and solid truth.

According to Roger Oakland, "When leaders who profess to be Christian intentionally or unintentionally hide God's word from people, the darkness this creates leads to a desire of spiritual encounters (experiences). In order to convince followers they are being spiritually fed by these Bible-depleted teachings, leaders implement all kinds of experience-based religious rituals and paraphernalia – thus, the reason that icons, candles, incense, liturgy, and the sacraments are deemed necessary for the emerging worship experience. (Oakland, Faith Undone, 2007).

This is highly prevalent in the Emergent Church as well as NAR. There is a huge movement out there to do away with the word of God altogether by saying that it's written by a bunch of racists!

When it comes to accepting small untruths, author Steve Quayle states, "95% truth plus five percent non-truth will damn you to Hell!" (Quayle, Steve Quayle Interview April 05 2018| Your King Is Coming, 2018). I know many people say, "Eat the meat and spit out the bones!" However, we cannot accept any half-truth. We must not allow the enemy to creep in at all.

Tree of Life

The other side is the Tree of Life. This tree is based on life and feeds off of Heaven's laws and precepts and is a narrower path. The Tree of Life will cost you your life. It will cost you everything. This tree is what branded Christianity because it is more Christ-like. Well the other kingdom is working hard to cast a bad light on this term because they want to flip the script on Christians. ***The Kingdom Come people believe in the word of God literally. They are fundamentalists.*** They believe the Book of Revelation is unfolding right now.

They believe trouble is on the horizon and therefore the other kingdom labels them "gloom and doom". They try to cast a bad light on them because they preach hell fire and brimstone, which keeps people focused on the consequences of sin and their separation from God. This fundamentalist group will receive great persecution in the days ahead. It did Jesus; why wouldn't it you?

Kingdom Now or Kingdom Come Theologies

It is obvious within the church world's battle over two kingdom beliefs and doctrines. The following graph is for the twokingdoms:

As you can see by this graphic, we have two different theologies present in the modern-day church. I must report that I was in the NAR theology up until I traveled the country last year and the Lord opened my eyes and showed me the sickness in the church.

The previous chapter was dedicated to reveal to you what that is. It wasn't until I started the TV show called THE CLARION CALL and begin to reveal the symptoms of what I saw on the road that I began researching and discovered the root of it all. This chapter is what I hope to reveal how these two different theologies are battling over the soul of America.

Through my research, my theory is that because of the Kingdom Now doctrine that it has caused the church to be sick. It has polluted the church to a terrible degree.

In addition, when you align with the Beast, you will get an easier path for your flesh in this life and no persecution. You will go with the flow and blend with the world.

IT'S CALLED THE TREE OF COMPROMISE.
GOD WILL SPEW YOU OUT OF HIS MOUTH.

Roger Oakland talks about the impact of this movement in his book, "It is indeed a 'new way of being Christians' and in every conceivable manner, it is striving to bring about a 'new reformation'. Without a doubt, it will have an 'impact on all churches' in the Western world and far beyond. For behind this new kind of church is a well-designed strategy and maneuver by the prince of this world, the enemy of our souls, to literally take apart the faith of millions –it will be nothing less than faith undone." (Oakland, Faith Undone, 2007)

I understand what he's saying because these groups cause people to trust in the experience of the senses and not the solid foundation of the word of God and the truths of God.

It truly is faith undone because they have so much power within the new revelation, they receive from God that they don't need faith anymore. They just take matters into their own hands.

What is Kingdom Now?

I realize now that Kingdom now really goes back to Rome because as we study the seven-mountain mandate, we discover that it's the major cultures of today (business, government, arts & entertainment, education, religion, etc.). The Roman Catholic Church wants to control all major cultures and mountains. They have their foot in almost every aspect. Being that they have partnered with most of religions in the Earth, they can help to setup the kingdom of this world for the Antichrist that is about to step on the scene. Think about it, if they can get everyone (all religions) to come in unity and take over the whole world with all the so-called Christians, then when it comes time, the savior of the world will step on the scene and will continue their bliss.

This also reflects the New Age ideology because you're all gods within.

****

You've got to ask yourself a huge question Bride, "Why are these groups partnering with the Pope? Catholic Church? Are they that dumb or ignorant or is it more selfish because of the doors they get opened and power, money, etc.? Why are they doing this? YOU MUST ASK YOURSELF THIS. THEN YOU MUST ASK YOURSELF, ARE YOUUUUUU GOING TO CONTINUE IN IT! You will answer to God for it too because when the judgment comes, whatever is attached to that heresy WILL GET JUDGED WITH THE SAME MEASURE – IGNORANT OR NOT!

Kingdom Now is a movement that has the basic tenants:

Kingdom Now theology is a branch of Dominion Theology which has had a following within Pentecostalism. It attracted attention in the late 1980s.

Kingdom Now theology states that although Satan has been in control of the world since the Fall, God is looking for people who will help him take back dominion. (Wikipedia, 2018)

I have found many descriptions of what this movement means on the internet and in books, but I believe this author has about the most accurate.

Kingdom Now theology is a theological belief within the Charismatic movement of Protestant Christianity, mainly in the United States. Kingdom Now proponents believe that God lost control over the world to Satan when Adam and Eve sinned. Since then, the theology goes, God has been trying to reestablish control over the world by seeking a special group of believers—known variously as "covenant people," "overcomers," or "Joel's army"— and that through these people, social institutions (including governments and laws) would be brought under God's authority. The belief is that, since believers are indwelt by the same Holy Spirit that indwelt Jesus, we have all authority in heaven and on the Earth; we have the power to believe for and speak into existence things that are not, and thus we can bring about the Kingdom Age.

Among the most controversial tenets of the theology is the belief that secular or non-Christian society will never succeed. Hence, Kingdom Now opposes a separation of church and state. Other beliefs include the idea that, as the Body of Christ, we are Christ. In other words, we have His divine nature.

Proponents of Kingdom Now teaching also don't believe in the rapture, which is explained away as a feeling of rapture or excitement when the Lord returns to receive the kingdom from our hands. In other words, everyone will be "caught up" emotionally when He returns.

Also, among the unbiblical beliefs is the idea that all prophecies regarding future Israel—both in the Old and New Testaments— actually apply to the church.

Kingdom Now theology sees the second coming of Jesus in two stages: first through the flesh of the believers (and in particular the flesh of today's apostles and prophets), and then in person to take over the kingdom handed to Him by those who have been victorious (the "overcomers"). Prior to the second coming, overcomers must purge the Earth of all evil influences. Kingdom Now claims that Jesus cannot return until all His enemies have been put under the feet of the church (including death, presumably).

Although there are people who believe in some, but not all, of Kingdom Now teachings, they do have in common the beliefs outlined above, all of which are outside of mainstream Christianity and all of which deny Scripture. First, the idea that God has "lost control" of anything is ludicrous, especially coupled with the idea that He needs human beings to help Him regain that control.

He is the sovereign Lord of the universe, complete and holy, perfect in all His attributes. He has complete control over all things—past, present and future—and nothing happens outside His command. Everything is proceeding according to His divine plan and purpose, and not one molecule is moving on its own accord. "For Jehovah of Hosts has purposed, and who shall reverse it? And His hand is stretched out, and who shall turn it back?" (Isaiah 14:27).

As for men having "the power to believe for and speak into existence things that are not," that power belongs to God alone, who doesn't take kindly to those who would attempt to usurp it from Him. "Remember this, and be a man; return it on your heart, O sinners. Remember former things from forever; for I am God, and no other is God, even none like Me, declaring the end from the beginning, and from the past things which were not done, saying, 'My purpose shall stand, and I will do all My pleasure'; calling a bird of prey from the east, the man of my purpose from a far country. Yes, I have spoken, I will also cause it to come; I have formed; yes, I will do it" (Isaiah 46:8-11). (Truth in Reality, 2012)

According to this article, Kingdom Now is a theology that states the following:

This age will end with a great revival causing the global triumph of Christianity with great signs and wonders convincing people of the truth of the Gospel as all other political and religious systems fail. *Prophecies relating to the restoration of Israel in the last days should in fact be applied to the church because the church has replaced Israel (or is the New Israel).* (Christians Together, 2011)

Here are a few of my interpretations of the way they believe:

Great revival is coming and will be in the middle of a great Utopia of peace. They believe that it will so big and glorious with miraculous signs and wonders. I do believe something is coming, but it will not be the way they are glossing it over with. I do believe a great move of God is coming, but it will not be in peace. It will be with great suffering.

However, considering the New Age Peace Plan (you all need to research that), it will "appear" as peace –it's their Golden Age – Dawning of a new day.

God is going to rain down his supernatural power upon all these superpowers and they will do miracles, signs and wonders more than Jesus did (which I do believe we are going to see this, but it will not be the way this group describes it. It will be in great suffering and nothing prideful about it at all). For instance, when you are persecuted and they're beating you, what will you do then? Look at the apostles/disciples back in Jesus' day. Every one of them were martyred except one and think of how they all reacted. Now we are all packing guns. (Not that I'm against guns – I'm not).

They are going to take over the seven mountains of culture and take over the world create a Utopia of "community". They do not believe that the Antichrist is about to step on the scene. Some believe that Jesus will return in each believer as they are manifested as this Joel's army. They will be "little gods" become one with Christ (universe).

They believe in the manifested sons of God. Although I do believe that we have the authority of Heaven and the inheritance from God, we cannot cross God's will. They believe they control everything because they have all the authority. There is a line we must consider – which is ourselves before God. We are not GREATER THAN OUR MASTER. For instance, if sickness or trouble comes, instead of rebuking the devil, we need to pray first to see if we've opened a door somewhere. It's not always the devil.

They believe that a new reformation is coming in huge magnitude. They believe a shift is coming in the Earth and they're partnering with the Pope to get there.

There is a great move to discredit the word "Christian" and "Christianity" because they want to do away with the old "order of things". They want to destroy the current system with a newer system of these superpowers who will now be in authority. This authority (apostle) is now much higher than just a pastor, thus they are the ones who oversee a whole city. The pastor should just sit down and shut up and let the apostle lead. However, did you know that all of this is not scriptural?

What Does Kingdom Now Believe?

In 2015 when I released my first book called *Mark of the Beast*, I had my first website client. This was my college major, so I was very happy! My book is from my master's degree college research paper from when I went to London on a study abroad class. I then converted it to a book in obedience to God. This book is about the human implantation device called RFID chip. In my theory, this chip is the mark of the beast and will cause you to be eternally damned to Hell. So, I just released this warning book to the Bride and realized that the client I had was preaching some strange doctrine.

I listened very closely and heard him explaining that they believe Jesus came back when He rose from the dead and there will be no tribulation or mark of the beast ahead, etc. In other words, they believe they were getting the Kingdom setup now for the Lord to return with His kingdom. (Basically, going straight into the millennial reign). I thought I was going to have a heart attack.

So, I confronted this pastor and said, "Sir, I just want to make sure I'm understanding your teaching right, can you explain to me what you mean by Kingdom Now?"

So, he invited me to his house for dinner and his wife and him tried to convert me to this new theology.

My heart was racing so hard (which later I learned that is the Holy Spirit letting me know I'm around evil).

I ended up telling this pastor that I can no longer work for him because I do not believe that way.

I explained to him that I am preparing the Bride for the Antichrist that is about to step on the scene and help them to not take the mark of the beast and be condemned to Hell! I was horrified that I was giving my services to a ministry that was teaching such heresy! However, he told me that Americans were not buying into it much, so he was setting up this huge network overseas (which my website helped him to do). Now it's everywhere!

So, years later I'm traveling all over the country and have been deeply involved with many ministries and they're all focused on Kingdom. I understood their concept in that we need to be kingdom-minded and focused on the bigger picture versus just focusing on ourselves or the individual ministries. It wasn't until God revealed to me last year what this is that I am now writing a book on it to warn the Body of Christ, so they get out of this mess and recognize that this is the Great Apostasy!

It's amazing how time rolled around and now I see this Kingdom Now doctrine all over the world! It's infiltrated America like a polluted stream.

It's tainted the Bride to an epic proportion. Most people do not even know they are blinded because on the outside it seems so right and pretty.

It's not until you step back and look at the fruit that you realize what you were in.

I consider a frog in a pot. Did you know a frog will not jump out of a cold pan as it is warming up? It will slowly boil to death.

This is what is happening in our country with this ecumenical movement, NAR and Emergent Church pollution crowding the rivers.

It just slowly creeped up on us and I was wondering, "What has happened in the church over the past twenty years that it just got so rotten?" Now I realize what happened. We slowly boiled in the filth. I hope we have time to jump out of the pot!

What they do Bride is when they are in "front of you" in conferences, live streams etc., they speak one way but when they are in big meetings with associations, etc., they have another plan. I'm telling you…please research their websites and what they believe in and who are they associating with. The wolf comes in sheep's clothing.

The Fruit of Kingdom Now Doctrine

A great example of the fruit is from one of the books by one of the main distributors of this doctrine, Bill Johnson. As this author states in her review of his book *When Heaven Invades Earth – a practical guide to a life of miracles.*

Moreover, Johnson envisions a spiritual kingdom where the Spirit receives more attention than Jesus (79, 89, 125) and the power of the gospel is some non-descript experience or manifestation (146). Whereas Romans 14:17 explains the manifestations of the kingdom as righteousness, peace, and joy in the Holy Spirit, Johnson speaks often of the kingdom in terms of overcoming sickness and controlling nature itself.

Once more, these delusions of grandeur may appeal to some, but they're not the manifestation of power that Paul describes in 1 Corinthians 2. Spiritual power brings new life, with its accompanying attributes of holiness, humility, love, and unity among diverse people. The kind of power Johnson offers is far less personal, and far more sensual. Therefore, I conclude it is unbiblical and sub-orthodox. (Schrock, 2017)

According to author Roger Oakland when writing about this Kingdom Now movement, he writes, "Let me speak very boldly here; if we are going to link hands with those who believe in another gospel or no gospel at all for the sake of establishing an Earthly, unified kingdom, we will not be building the kingdom of God. (Oakland, Faith Undone, 2007)

Kingdom Now Twists the Word of God

In Bill Johnson's book, he's relating to his readers that in addition to the word of God, we need to have experience with God. There is nothing wrong with this – per say.

However, in his definition however, he takes it a little too far, "Anything I can get from the Word without God will not change my life. It is closed to ensure that I remain dependent on the Holy Spirit." (Johnson, When Heaven Invades Earth, 2003) He keeps his Bible closed to hear from the Holy Spirit? This is divination people! Bill is explaining in this part of the book, "Bible teachers are to instruct in order to explain what they just did or are about to do. Those who restrict themselves to mere words limit their gift and may unintentionally lead believers to pride by increasing knowledge without an increased awareness of God's presence and power.

It's in the trenches of Christ-like ministry that we learn to become totally dependent upon God. Moving in the impossible through relying on God short-circuits the development of pride." (Johnson, When Heaven Invades Earth, 2003)

He is basically telling the church that it is more important to walk listening a spirit than it is in the word of God. See this type of thinking suggests that the spirit supersedes the word. It does not. They flow together.

The whole point of Kingdom Now teaching is that experience supersedes the word of God. It's more about experience than the mandates of the word of God. In other words, they think we are "limiting" God by just keeping it in the restraints of the written.

I could give you many more, but I don't have enough room in these books! I chose Bill and Bethel Church as examples because of the magnitude of their ministry.

How Did All This Begin?

Through my research I discovered that it all boils down to the Roman Catholic Church. See, the Roman Catholic Church is the main group behind all the powers of the world. They are the great whore of Babylon as stated in the Bible.

> *Revelation 17 1 And there came one of the seven angels which had the seven vials, and talked with me, saying unto me, Come hither; I will shew unto thee the judgment of the great whore that sitteth upon many waters:*

2 With whom the kings of the Earth have committed fornication, and the inhabitants of the Earth have been made drunk with the wine of her fornication. 3 So he carried me away in the spirit into the wilderness: and I saw a woman sit upon a scarlet coloured beast, full of names of blasphemy, having seven heads and ten horns. 4 And the woman was arrayed in purple and scarlet colour, and decked with gold and precious stones and pearls, having a golden cup in her hand full of abominations and filthiness of her fornication: 5 And upon her forehead was a name written, Mystery, Babylon The Great, The Mother Of Harlots And Abominations Of The Earth. 6 And I saw the woman drunken with the blood of the saints, and with the blood of the martyrs of Jesus: and when I saw her, I wondered with great admiration. 7 And the angel said unto me, Wherefore didst thou marvel? I will tell thee the mystery of the woman, and of the beast that carrieth her, which hath the seven heads and ten horns. 8 The beast that thou sawest was, and is not; and shall ascend out of the bottomless pit, and go into perdition: and they that dwell on the Earth shall wonder, whose names were not written in the book of life from the foundation of the world, when they behold the beast that was, and is not, and yet is. 9 And here is the mind which hath wisdom. The seven heads are seven mountains, on which the woman sitteth.

In verse nine I can't help wondering if those seven mountains are the NAR's mandate of the seven mountains.

Think about it. They are saying that the Christians must take over the seven mountains of culture and then we will conquer the world. Does this not sound like the Beast? This mandate that they are proclaiming is not in scripture at all.

Then when they try to say that they must prepare the Earth for Jesus to return, that is not true as well. God has already spoken to us about the future. I'll get into this later.

Let me show you this graph I made based upon other graphs I found on the internet.

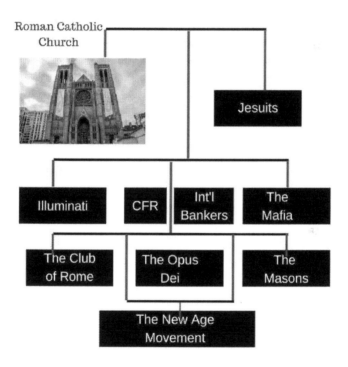

Great wars have happened over the years over religion. According to author Roger Oakland, the Roman Catholic Church wants all the religions to come under the Mother Church again (Roman Catholic Church). (Oakland, Faith Undone, 2007).

The Roman Catholic (RC) church considers us "separated brethren" (the Protestant church). (Oakland, Faith Undone, 2007)

They have infiltrated it from the inside out. This began in 1948.

Isn't that funny that it began the same year that Israel became a nation?

The Faith Challenge

Another characteristic I see about these groups is the lack of endurance. This microwave generation wants things now and do not want to wait. Faith in God includes faith in his timing. We must be willing to wait and have patience for God to answer our prayers. In the older generation they know how to tarry and travail. In truth, this is how God expects us to be. We pray, then trust and obey.

I think this is a revelation about the Kingdom NOW doctrine. As a Christian we must tarry and wait. This requires faith. Faith walks blindly trusting God. It requires that we trust in the Lord with the unknown. We trust in him to carry out the right answer. I counsel people that we love him when he says no and when he says yes. We trust in Him. This movement does not do this. This is how:

Courts of Heaven – They want control of their lives, so they will astral-project by taking their souls out of their bodies and travel to the third heaven (which is an occult practice). Instead of waiting on God to answer this prayer, they want control by taking things in their own hands and go fight for what they want. This also takes away their own accountability because it's a pride issue. They think they have authority to bypass Jesus and his rules in answering prayers. This requires lack of faith. By them leaving their bodies in astral projection, they leave their souls open for possession by demons.

Seven Mountain Mandate – This is their idea of taking over the world by Christians. Although I do agree that Christians should get involved in every aspect of life, I do not agree that we are take power of all the different pillars of our society. Don't get me wrong, if God advanced a person to the top, then it should be through humility. This belief patterns what I call the Preacher Pyramid – where it's top heavy. All the power is at the top. It's another form of power control. Remember the servant? Where is the faith in this strategy?

Contemplative Prayer – This is a New Age practice. These groups seek after extra-biblical experience. For instance, the following a pattern of chants, repetitive words and shutting your mind down, etc. What faith does this require? They present a vision in their head and sometimes astral project to another realm that they should not be in. Why do we seek to do the extra when it goes outside the biblical bounds? Why? Because if not it requires faith. Faith means you talk to God even when you don't hear him back or see him or feel him or any other type of manifestation. I'll get more into this later…

Prosperity Gospel – This is like I said earlier where people will be greedy with money. Where is the ministry's faith in God to supply without having to manipulate the Bride? They will answer to God for this mess. As I reiterated earlier, God does want us prosperous and in health, but not to where it affects our heart and greed sets in. Many people have quit churches over the years because of this. It's an embarrassment to the Christian faith. They're really pimping out the anointing for money. Manipulation is as the sin of witchcraft.

I recently received an email, and this is a great example, "It's coming for you: an anointing for abundance, angelic intervention, deliverance from affliction — and much, much more! Sow your Passover Offering now as a seed of faith for seven amazing Passover anointings.

Passover season is when Jesus did the most miracles while He walked this Earth. It is a season we can expect miracles.

This is like paying for anointings. I understand sowing and reaping, etc. But, I read in Jeremiah how God will judge the land if we neglect the widows and the poor. I've been in meetings where I could not get prayed for by the speaker because I did not have money. Not good.

Positivity Preaching – When these groups preach that sin does not hold them back from God, and only preach things that build up man's flesh, it requires no faith to continue. They can continue in their behaviors without consequences. If they do not like the way something is going, instead of trusting God, they just speak something positive and ignore the danger signs right in front of them. They only look at the good stuff and not face the tough things. This is a New Age practice as well. They have the mindset that "All is Bliss in this World". It is a very misleading concept. No faith required here because you do not face challenges. They avert and avoid them. It's examining your heart. When calamity comes up, we should seek God and we may need to repent – not just cover it up by flowery words. It's called being HONEST with God.

Follow Signs, Miracles & Wonders – What faith is needed when you can always see the manifestations of God, or some type of manifestation anyway. When a minister says they have the manifestations, people will flock to them.

Why? Are there transformations taking place? Are drunks being set free? Are prostitutes being released from the bondages of Hell? Are people at the alter crying and being delivered? No! They're all too busy oozing and aweing over the signs. The Bible talks about this as a wicked generation that follows the signs! (Matt. 16:4). What faith do you need when you can see and touch and experience it right then?

There are many more examples, but I wanted to show you that most of these groups that have tapped into this worldly beast, they have regressed from the following since they went that way:

Less in the Bible – many are not seeking their knowledge out of the Bible, but rather out of experience. They are teaching people that we no longer need it or that it is an antiquated book. As I quoted earlier from Bill Johnson of Bethel Church, "He's wanting to raise up a generation of people who will want to learn to live from the presence of God as opposed to living merely from the principles of God. And that's a big deal. Because in the principles there is success, but from the presence there is no failure". (Johnson, A Mess- Heidi Baker - Bill Johnson - Rolland Baker - Bethel Redding, 2017) This belief once again stresses experience over truth. This is very dangerous.

Adoption of New Age & Occult Practices – quantum physics, astral-projection, visualization, SOZO prayers, labyrinth prayers, grave-sucking, destiny cards and all the other satanic mess. This is because the Tree of Knowledge of Good and Evil. They want MORE at all costs.

Serving Others & Servanthood – With these groups it is about power and position. The self-proclaimed apostles and prophets have appointed themselves over pastors and thus they want to shut churches down and overtake cities and communities. They want to override the old system and bring in their system because they are superior now like superheroes. They have super-human power through Dominionism and the 7-M Mandate, so they are more powerful than anyone else.

Obeying the 10 Commandments & God's Word – They think because they have all this extra-biblical knowledge that they are above God's boring original rules. If God tells us not to touch the unclean thing because he wants his bride pure; this group cannot do that because they want more power and authority. They want to be the head literally instead of the servant.

Suffering Like Christ – This group does not believe that Christians should suffer at all. They believe that with all their power and authority they will just take control over all their situations, go to the 3rd heavens and declare a winning on their behalf.

They will speak to all those mountains (even if it's their own self) and tell them to get out of their life. They take all matter into their own hands, so they do not have to suffer. If they get persecuted, well they will just water down the gospel so that others won't be offended and include all in heaven (inclusion) – even if the word disagrees with them. They believe that if someone is suffering that something is wrong with them. They don't understand that God's own word says that we will suffer as Christ suffered. If he was persecuted then we will be too because if they hate him, then they will hate us. (Acts 9:16, Rom. 8:17, Rom. 8:36, 2 Cor 1:17, 2 Cor. 11:23, Phil. 3:10, 2 Tim. 2:12, Heb. 11:25, James 5:10, 1 Pet. 2:20, 1 Pet. 3:14, 1 Pet. 4:16, 1 Pet. 5:10, Matt. 5:11, Matt. 10:22, Matt. 10:39, Matt. 19:29, 1 Cor. 4:10). There are many more scriptures. Basically, these groups do not want to suffer in the manner that God so requires.

Why? Because of wrong teaching and pride. Our culture has become so accustomed to having to look like the Jones' and that you're not successful until you're rich with a beautiful home, nice car, etc. It's backwards actually. You know Bride that you can have all those things if the things do not have you. It's a big difference. Are you manipulating people and things just to keep those things? Are you telling God's people as you send a sexy picture on Facebook and telling people, "You will receive a financial blessing to the first 20 people who share this picture." It showed her cleavage with a spirit of perversion all over her. She had a ton of people encouraging her! God help the church.

The Worldly Kingdom Now & Pope's Kingdom

I must mention this here because you've heard me reference it before. Bride, it's all the same. Both kingdoms they're building is for the Antichrist stepping on the scene. Jesus commands us to witness to people and help them to not be deceived and to prepare for his coming. He wants them to obey him and to fulfill their destinies on Earth. They can't do that if they must partner with the Beast to achieve it. The Pope is building his kingdom and any ministry that partners with that is contributing to his kingdom. The globalists are working on world unity at same time. It's all together! Think about what I revealed about Iran. – The Golden Age of Peace. It's common sense.

Which Kingdom Will You Choose?

In the Kingdom Come movement it requires everything. God is not playing around. The end of times is here, and we must choose this day whom we will serve. The Lord is separating the wheat from the tares and it is our time to decide.

Are we going to go against the flow of this movement and follow truth and give up all for Jesus or are we going to go with the flow which promotes self and instant answers? Let me make this very clear:

Kingdom Come:

Luke 14:33 So likewise, whosoever he be of you that forsaketh not all that he hath, he cannot be my disciple.

- Lay down your life and possibly be martyred
- Speak truth and stand up for truth amidst persecution and your reputation being attacked falsely, etc.
- Preparing for the end of time and Jesus' return
- Separating yourself from the world and disconnecting from all idols to include:
  - New Age
  - Occult
  - Worldly Influences such as Yoga, essential oils, contemplative prayer, labyrinths, Reiki, eastern mysticism, necromancy, tattoos, piercings, worldly music, and all other Satanic-influenced worldly things.
  - Self-Worship
  - Ministries who mix with other religions
  - Obedience to God and willing to give to others or him
- Waiting patiently on God to move and trusting that He is in control. We do not control him or our lives. He does.
- Realize that we are God's children and servants.

- When we die, we pray to hear him say, "Well done
- thy good and faithful servant."
- On Earth we will serve one master or the other.
- We must realize that we cannot touch the unclean thing, or we will be judged with the unclean thing. It's like we're connected to the rotten vine. We must purify ourselves and remove the blot/wrinkle/taint/sin.

This is the Kingdom Now:

- Prior to the second coming, overcomers must purge the Earth of all evil influences. Kingdom Now claims that Jesus cannot return until all His enemies have been put under the feet of the church (including death, presumably)." (KOHLER, 2016)
- Others of them have extreme views on God's grace and have no concept of God's hatred toward sin and the requirement of repentance and holiness. (Odle, The Polluted Church; From Rome to Kansas City, 2012)
- Sadly, most of them will not listen to any voice of caution. They are consumed with chasing a "miracle" or give them a word of "prophecy'. They just do not realize that they are being polluted and opening doors to demons that can destroy them. (Odle, The Polluted Church; From Rome to Kansas City, 2012)
- Working to bring about Utopia on Earth through global and religious unity is futile….nowhere in scripture is the notion supported that there will be a kingdom without tears, pain, poverty, and suffering until Jesus Christ physically returns and establishes it Himself. (Oakland, Faith Undone, 2007)

- One of these satanic devices is to pervert the aims of the church. He deludes church leaders into thinking that the main purpose of the church today is not so much to save individuals out of society as to save society, not so much to save souls as to save the bodies of men, not so much to save men out of a community as to save men and manhood in the community. The world, not the individual, is the subject of redemption. (Bounds, 1984)

- The Kingdom of God is the place, or the location, where the King resides, right? And if we can all agree that Jesus is our King, then He resides in our hearts when we accept Him as our Savior and the Holy Spirit takes up residence in us. The location of the Kingdom is spiritual! We, as human beings, cannot establish an Earthly Kingdom for Him and then hand the keys over to Him ... nowhere is that expressed in the Bible! (KOHLER, 2016)

  - Peter 2:18-22 "For when they speak great swelling words of vanity, they allure through the lusts of the flesh, through much wantonness, those that were clean escaped from them who live in error. While they promise them liberty, they themselves are the servants of corruption: for of whom a man is overcome, of the same is he brought in bondage. For if after they have escaped the pollutions of the world through the knowledge of the Lord and Saviour Jesus Christ, they are again entangled therein, and overcome, the latter end is worse with them than the beginning. For it had been better for them not to have known the way of righteousness, than, after they have known it, to turn from the holy commandment delivered unto them. But it is happened unto them according to the true proverb, the dog is turned to his own vomit again; and the sow that was washed to her wallowing in the mire."

- Seeking after signs more than the truth. Matthew 16:2-4 "He answered and said unto them, when it is evening, ye say, It will be fair weather: for the sky is red. And in the morning, it will be foul weather today: for the sky is red and lowering. O ye hypocrites, ye can discern the face of the sky; but can ye not discern the signs of the times? A wicked and adulterous generation seeketh after a sign; and there shall no sign be given unto it, but the sign of the prophet Jonas. And he left them and departed."

- When God instructed Moses in the building of the tabernacle, God gave specific instructions on how to use the pure gold and pure silver and the precious stones. God required the genuine articles. Because the purity of precious metal and stones reflect His own value and worth. God is repulsed by counterfeits and of anything impure. So, when we examine the scriptures as the Bereans did, would we find a God there who would manifest his glory with imitation gold dust and plastic gems? Unfortunately, a lot of pastors and leaders have been caught up in whatever it takes to win the people, even in the name of deception.

- Leviticus 10:1 And a spiritual adulterer is one turns his or her focus from the person and work of Jesus Christ to seek spectacular displays in His name.

- Follow experience more than the word.

- The seven (7) mountain mandate where they take over the world.

- Not preparing the church for Jesus' return. They're actually, preparing for the Golden Age of New Age Peace.

- One does not have to wade very far into the waters of Dominionism before encountering an old Hermetic heresy that heaven and Earth can become united, as illustrated by the quotation above. This doctrine is now rampantly taught throughout the New Age Movement and the New Apostolic Reformation, as well as mission organizations and political left and right Dominionists movements. This doctrine is key because it creates a point of synthesis and syncretism between many many religious groups, Christian and non-Christian. It is also easy to work with. By simply changing an emphasis in language, one can begin to alter the traditional doctrine to include a new theology. But the theology isn't new. It is old. (Herescope, 2007)

- Blends New Age in with their teachings – This advertisement is from a group partnered with Bethel Church. This group is on an island called Byron Bay. This school – NAOITH College educates people in this mess and sends them all over the world to infect others:

NAIOTH PROPHETIC SCHOOL –
T U E S D A Y N I G H T - 22 AUGUST

MARIA MASON will be teaching on:
Mystics & Prayer Temperaments.
Come join us for an awesome night of glory,
worship and teaching.

Our study this week is a fascinating way of seeing our individual temperaments and the intersection with our prayer styles. The apostle John was of course an introvert who thought deeply and experienced God in visions. Peter on the other hand was an extrovert who was less inclined to think and more inclined to feel. If he had done the Myer Briggs test he probably would've been a ESFP! We will look at the way four different Mystics, Thomas, Augustine, St Francis and Ignatius, approached their communion with God. We will see how our differing sacred pathways reveal a greater way for connecting to God in our lives as we understand our own particular temperaments and unique ways of connecting to God. Please bring your journal or notebook. (NAIOTH COLLEGE, 2017)

Please notice how they are teaching these students out of Catholic teaching and sources. These people – Thom as Augustine, St. Francis and Ignatius are all mystics. This is the same type of theology that IHOP teaches their people.

Random Pic

In picture is President Trump with Army 2019

Theological Breakdown of Difference
of Two Kingdoms

KN Kingdom NOW	KC Kingdom Come
KN wants to have UNITY at the cost of compromise with others who are involved in idolatry, cults, Roman Catholic Church and is ecumenical.	KC wants UNITY based on truth only. Believes in Eph 4:3 – unity is based on the spirit and word. Then Eph 4:13 declares unity based on doctrine.
KN is based upon an amillennial or postmillennial model. They believe Christ is coming back to a cleaned-up world.	KC believes the Book of Revelation is about to unfold with the Antichrist and believes in pre-millennial.
KN gives the perception that they believe that either Jesus is ONLY coming back after they take over the world or he's not coming back, and they are walking gods on the Earth	KC believes Jesus is coming soon, either pre-mid-post. It doesn't matter when he is coming, as long as we believe he IS coming.
KN believes in the prosperity gospel and promotes that wealth and material things is a sign of the blessings of God on your life. Many will teach not to hang around the less fortunate. Go UP and leave the down.	KC believes that what you have is God's and He knows all. Obedience is the Key to wealth. There are many ways to be wealthy. Time is wealth, Family, Love, Friends, etc. It's not in material things. Lay up your treasures in Heaven.

KN believes that we need to save society versus the individual which is why they focus on titles such as the 5-fold. It's about the power and position. They want to be ON TOP of the mountain.	KC believes that we are the children of God and servants. This is top priority because GOD knows all. He sees the big picture. I don't need to go to the courts in the 3rd heaven and astral project my soul out of my body to achieve my own desires. I HAVE FAITH.
KN believes they're either little gods, equal, friend or Jesus Himself. They are not called to serve; they are not servants. Therefore, they do Courts of Heaven, etc. is so that they can battle their own case and keep things in their own hands.	
KN believes that the Great Commission isn't to convert or save individual Christians, it is to change society to form a worldly kingdom. They believe that we should all be universalists and a "community". We shouldn't think that because we're saved that Jesus is the ONLY way.	KC believes the Great Commission is for the transformation of INDIVIDUAL SOULS AND REQUIRES TRANSFORMATION OF PEOPLE, NOT CITIES. Jesus is the ONLY way to salvation.
KN believes in partnering with other religions and cultivating that in their own services – meetings and lives. They believe in bringing the world in	KC believes in being bold and separating themselves from the unclean and unholy. They believe in not "touching the unclean thing". They believe

so that they can be "relevant and cool" to the younger generation. They believe in watering down the gospel in order to not offend others and to "soften the blow"	that God is worthy all by himself and we do not need to partner with Satan and his devices in order for people to get saved. The truth will always set people free.
KN believes that we have full dominion on the Earth and Jesus has paid all the price for sin, thus we do not need to consider sin again. Jesus took care of it; even future sins. It's a once-saved-always-saved, pluralistic belief.	KC believes that Jesus will restore the Earth when he returns. Yes, he paid the price but we must keep our sins under repentance and be an overcomer
KN believes that they must takeover these mountains and be on top, yet they criticize the church because the pastors have it wrong being on the top. They're telling the traditional church to flip the pyramid, yet they are wanting to be the head now and put everyone else under them	KC believes that God loves his church and we need to repent and allow God to fulfill his hands in the Earth as we fulfill the great commission, which is seeking souls and transforming families and lives. We are not called to change systems, but people.

KN considers the word "Kingdom" over "Christianity". They're actually painting a bad light on the word Christianity. Kingdom = unity with everyone – the kingdom on Earth. Throw doctrine aside and come together to help humanity = social justice. Same is happening in the world such as IRAN and Jerusalem – preparing for NOW.	KC believes in the Kingdom of God, however, it's inside of us. Jesus tells us when we go somewhere that we bring the kingdom with us. We are carriers of the kingdom. The bible doesn't say the planet will be a restored kingdom for Jesus, rather it does say it is preparing for THE KINGDOM OF THE ANTICHRIST!
KN has made an idol out of social justice. It tries to solve the problems of mankind by fleshly needs. However, partnering with the world and other religions to do it is not the answer.	KC believes that in order to help a person, it must be met with inner help. They need salvation, healing, deliverance, etc. Putting a band aid on it is not going to help but momentarily!
KN believes that sin does not bother them and they actually hate talking about it because it is negative. Jesus took care of that on the cross and they shouldn't worry about it. They are not about correction or self-evaluation	KC believes that we are the children of God and God corrects us, rebukes us, chastises us and causes us to repent and change. Sin crouches at the door so we must be aware and alert.

KN believes that you cannot talk against a leader or you are a terrible person. They demand extreme loyalty. However, they preach against the traditional church role of people's loyalty to their own pastors. They want everyone in their network and they want everyone to pay them	KC believes that yes we do cherish our roles with who we serve, however, we are to seek God for ourselves and if a false prophet is harming the sheep, then we have every right to speak against the heresy. We love truth more than political correctness. We're loyal to
all this money to buy their books and go to their conferences and pay monthly dues. We can preach all the heresy we want because people don't read the bible and check what we say because they are EXPERIENCING SOMETHING.	God. They trust in the word of God over any person place or thing.
KN believes that the Holy Spirit trumps the Bible so we don't need it anymore except a verse here and there. Our experience overrides doctrine and fundamentalist-thinking people.	KC believes the spirit always matches the word of God. They go together. The word of God must be verified and confirm the spirit because many false spirits out there. We trust the word of God!

KN believes that it's OK to be elite with such titles as Apostles, Prophets, Tribes, Community, etc. and they often teach others that everyone else is "toxic", "Jezebel", and definitely provides the impression that they are superior to everyone else (from the dominion theology) – They think they are "above"	KC believes that we are servants in the kingdom. We are to prefer others above ourselves. We have no problem being on the streets with the homeless, the drug-addicts, elderly, etc. We are to be carriers of God's light to humanity and help them to get out of the darkness instead of us trying to shine brighter than everyone else in self-promotion
KN believes that they can have extra-biblical revelation even if it contradicts the old written word of God that man only interpreted. They feel like the extra knowledge was held until this generation and they are more special because they are privy to this glory manifestations	KC measures everything by the word. Although God is supernatural and can do things outside of the realm of just what is written, it will not be out of God's character. This is where the difference is. Why would God manifest gems, gold dust, feathers, etc., and it not help people? How is this helping the kingdom as a whole? Can we sell it and help the poor? Is it real? Many that has been tested (almost all) is all fake.

KC most definitely believes in the infilling of the Holy Ghost and manifestations. However, the manifestations are holy. They do not bring reproach or cause people to discern goofiness such as barking, howling, contorting their bodies, etc. Yes, the HS is free to express himself but it always brings glory to Jesus and not to the person or the devil. It's one thing to travail in prayer where you sound like you're having a baby (deep intercession) versus screaming like you're in agonizing pain and being tortured. We must discern.	KN transfers the Kundalini spirit to others as it mocks the Holy Spirit. This is a Hindu/New Age spirit. It brings feelings of euphoria and bliss and unnatural joy. It also manifests as violent jerks, shakes, levitation, etc. This spirit can also manifest in the gold dust, jewels, etc. The Hindus and New Age religion all heal people by this spirit as well. Kundalini is a serpent spirit that runs up the base of the spine and activates the Chakras and opens the 3rd eye, which is where the "bliss" comes in. It's unholy. The difference is the fruit. Always judge by the fruit.

KN says they LOVE everyone and very inclusive of others and tolerant and no offense to others. This is a false love. If you watch the old hippies or the New Age people when they're high…that's what the spirit looks like on a lot of people	KC says Jesus' love divides. It is a sword. It cuts. The truth hurts. Truth is real love. Love is patient, kind and all that; however, it's also truth which is the justice side of God. Jesus' love never tolerates sin or devils
KN can operate out of a Cain spirit as well. Some are operating out of Kundalini which is where the hippie-side is, but many in the NAR operate out of the Cain spirit. The Cain spirit is the one that killed Abel. It is the arrogant pompous one. Study this out. This will also be one of the spirit that kills "Fundamental Christians" one day because they're already turning people against that term Christians. So, one day they will kill their "brother" like Cain did with Abel. This is also why they want to be at the top of the mountain and in control (titles – apostles, prophets, networks, etc.)	KC is considered fundamentalist Christians because they believe the word of God to be truthful and literal. They are considered the "old school" people. They are the antiquated ones who are out of touch with the postmodern world. This is why the KN believes they need more world in the church and needs to "blend" with other cultures because we are too "stiff and right-winged, fanatical, and defined by one leading Catholic Priest – spiritual terrorist!" So, yes, this group will be the ones martyred in the very near future.

KN people believe that you should not suffer. They believe that if you are suffering then something's wrong with you. You're not doing something right. Although your life is upright before God and you're bearing fruit – they're measurement of success is by material things being that they believe in the prosperity gospel and sell their prophecies, etc.	KC people know that you will suffer as Christ suffered. See, the KN people do not go through persecution because they are so busy "blending in" with the world that they are not on Satan's radar. They may think they are being persecuted, but it may just be God convicting them and they're not listening because they're prideful and stubborn. Stiff-necked. The KC people obey God no matter what God desires. They recognize the cost of the call
KN believes that there is no need to fear God because they are equal or they are either a god themselves. They do not fear death because some of them don't even believe in a literal Hell anymore. Because they believe once-saved always-saved or that grace covers all and no need to worry, they are OK in God's eyes	KC knows that fearing God is the key to wisdom. They fear God and are very aware of their sin nature, thus they are open to correction, rebuke and chastisement. They want God to keep them in line because they are the children of God and servants.

KN does not believe they are servants, they are FRIENDS. (We cannot be above our master, and yes we are a friend of God...but servant first)	KC believes we are servants and the children of God. We know our place in the kingdom and we walk by faith
KN wants to have the extra-biblical experiences like visuals, contemplative prayer, courts of heaven, labyrinths, etc., so that they can see and touch and not need faith. KN has demonic visitations classified by them as angels. Todd Bentley is famous for his female angel named Emma. There are no female angels in the Bible. This is demonic.	KC realizes that when we pray and partner with Heaven that what God does from there is up to Him. We say, "If it be thy will." Who can know the perfect will of God all the time? We trust Him that He sees all, knows all and loves us and will take care of us. He's always looking out for our good. In other words, he knows the big picture. We do not.
KN mixes with New Age activities such as Yoga, Essential Oils, Labyrinths, Contemplative Prayer, Tarot Cards, Palm Readings, Energy Transfers, Holistic Healing, etc.	KC knows that God hates divination. Most of that is divination. God hates mixing and requiring any other thing to find out about the future, mystical, mysticism, etc. NO!

KN eats their own fruit. They are so hungry for more experiences and knowledge about the supernatural, that they literally go from meeting to meeting wanting more "words" and knowledge and not ever give it away. They eat their own fruit.	KC believes that God gives us infillings so that we can GIVE IT AWAY. It's not for us to keep or hoard. It is for others. It is not self-seeking.
KN eats off the Tree of Knowledge of Good and Evil – this means they hunger after the supernatural and knowledge more than the boundaries preset by God	KC eats off the Tree of Life. They understand that we have limitations and boundaries set by God for a reason. We are not trying to build a Tower of Babel

I could say so much more, but I only have so many pages in this book, LOL. I hope you get the point. Kingdom NOW means just that.

Being that my major is Corporate Communications, I understand target audiences, setting the stage for the event, advertising, logos, symbols, etc. I've watched how this group conducts UNITY events. This is one thing about the NAR – Kingdom NOW people is that they do unified events for many reasons. Granted, not everyone in this group believes this or does this, but I'm talking about the powers-that-be and their targets and goals. This is based upon my research AND being a part of it for the past five years traveling all over the United States and serving many ministries.

HOW TO KNOW IF YOU HAVE KUNDALINI AWAKENING

According to this New Age website, "You begin to start seeing and feeling energy around yourself and others. This can manifest in many different forms, the more common occurrences:

- Seeing orbs of light within peripheral vision
- Light flashes
- Prickly or tingling sensations, like the sensation of static electricity
- A feeling of something deep flowing through you like the ebb and flow of water aka kundalini flow
- Pressure in the head or a sudden sensation of *pushing*
- A pulsing, tremor or twitching sensation.
- A sensation like a change in altitude or barometric pressure
- A shift in consciousness like an abrupt shift in mood or clarity
- Tracers or after-images amongst objects or auras around people
- Tingling or vibrating sensation from head to toe
- Feeling unexplainable warmth in the hands or feet {signs of a natural healer!}
- A sudden chill, random goosebumps or cold feeling. {sign of releasing energy}
- Swirling orbs of light within the sky or clouds
- Seeing colors of frequency (commonly mistaken with the disorder synesthesia).
- The blue pearl/orb appearing in your vision aka seeing your consciousness in manifested form. (Aliff, Symptoms of Kundalini Awakening, 2018)

On her website she talks about many other symptoms that I've seen many of my friends have such as obsessions with numbers, emotional upheaval, feeling lost/confused/having an identity crisis, dark nights of the soul, strongly feeling and seeing energy, increase in psychic abilities (prophetic words, etc.), encountering past-life memories, flashes into other realities, panic/anxiety attacks, zero tolerance for negative people or lower-energy people, memory problems/fog, vertigo, vivid dreams/prophetic dreams, meditation, being more introspective, frequent headaches/central forehead pains or pain in the temple, chest symptoms, heart palpitations, ear ringing, natural spiritual high, diet changes, extreme sensitivity to crowds/loud environments, body tingling from head to toe, change in sleep patterns, electronics don't like you, changes in weight, looking younger, hypersensitivity and skin reactions, detoxification, wanting to release the old you, begin questioning God and divinity, teachers appear everywhere, the desire for spiritual and material abundance, feeling a deeper connection to the universe/ God/resonance of your own divinity, looking into career fields of healing/alternative medicine/holistic practice of your dream job, new sense of oneness, integration with the universe, living your purpose, and others. (Aliff, Symptoms of Awakening, 2018)

This really does answer a nagging thought I've had about the charismatics. Why do they go from meeting to meeting seeking words, (prophecies), miracles signs and wonders so much? Now I know. Once they get a high from this they continually go back.

Bride don't forget that I am Pentecostal and I do believe in the gifts of the spirit. I encourage you to do the research yourself. Type in *Kundalini* on your search engine and on YouTube.

5

Ministries & the

One World Religion

Ecumenical Gathering & Covenant Churches

The Bible talks about a one world religion coming together in the last days and describes her as the great Whore of Babylon. I believe so far, I've provided enough proof scripturally and common sense- wise. The whore cheats on God. It's false, fake and ungodly.

According to *ChristianProphecy.org*, "The Christian leaders who are advocating tolerance to the point of embracing apostasy are going to triumph soon, at least temporarily. The Bible makes that clear. Just as "one world" thought is dominating the political and economic scenes today; it has captivated the thinking of both Catholic and Protestant leaders regarding religion." Dr. Reagan explains in this article how this apostasy is blending the different religions and how they're lying to people proclaiming that it is all the same God. He ends this article by stating, "I believe the harlot church of Revelation 17 will most likely be an amalgamation of the world's pagan religions, including apostate Protestants, under the leadership of the Catholic Church." (Reagan, 2018)

I could not agree more about Revelation 17! I heard a minister say the other day that it might be Israel as the Great Harlot because she is the capitol of the world for LGBTQ (ultimate perversion) and will be the ones who will kill the true church (Noahide Laws). I also think it may be the United States because we are the most powerful country on the planet and we control everyone. We are the strong arm of the UN as well. We monitor every country, give aid to them, etc. We have also peddled the LGBTQ across the world, alongside Israel. We are both on the UN LGBTI committee. So, the covenant that our country has with God causes me to consider that maybe it is us. Another thought agrees with that lady in the previous page who thinks it is the Catholic Church. They are the ones who are causing everyone to merge across the world in the one world religion so we will see.

Former nun, Charlotte Kepler, explains in her life story after serving 23 years in a convent and being tortured, which finally led to escaping, "The Holy Bible declares in the Book of Revelation, Seventeenth Chapter, that this Babylon (Rome) is a whore with whom the kings of the earth have committed fornication, and the inhabitants of the earth have been made drunk with the wine of her fornication. It describes her as being arrayed in purple and scarlet colors, decked with gold, precious stones and pearls and having a golden cup in her handful of abominations and filthiness of her fornication. Upon her head is written, "Mystery, Babylon the Great, the Mother of Harlots and Abominations of the Forth. She's drunken with the blood of the saints and with the blood of the martyrs of Jesus The Bible declares, in picturesque form, that Babylon sets on seven mountains." (Keckler, 1999).

Also, according to this nun, they're very torturous, "I have seen a little Nun strapped to a chair under a fountain of water.

The faucet would be turned on to allow one drop o£ water at a time to fall on her head, the most vital part where the brain is located. This would continue for hours before she was released. I have seen some Nuns whose eyes became crossed. Others went raving mad and were placed in chains in the dungeon below, while others crumpled to the floor when released. I've also seen a red rubber cap very similar to an ordinary bathing cap placed on a Nun for punishment.

In a minute and a half, she was on the floor writhing and foaming at the mouth like a mad dog. If left on for over three minutes, she was a corpse. I cannot describe the mechanism of that cap as I never had the privilege of inspecting it.

But I have worn it and it felt like a thousand wires were piercing my brain. The mental torture was excruciating. Convents are un-American, ungodly, inhuman and horribly corrupting.

The Siberian labour camps cannot equal the Convents that have enslaved beautiful young girls, tortured their brains, broken their bodies, subjected them to the lusts of evil priests, and buried them in lime pits. (Keckler, 1999)

Ex-nun Charlotte Keckler writes of her belief of the Great Whore again, "How grateful I am, after having been in a convent and saw the Mother Harlot and the Tiber fulfilling Revelation's prophecy, to be delivered from the convent. I came out to shockingly find a world fighting against, and at the same time, embracing the beast of Communism (Revelation 17), for a judgment in which God the righteous Judge shall judge the world (Acts 17:31). (Keckler, 1999) Through my research, my theory is that because of the ecumenical movement, emergent church and Kingdom Now doctrine that it has caused the church to be sick. It has polluted the church to a terrible degree. I hope to explain it to you in this chapter.

Let's Examine Some Ministries Partnering w/OWR

Let's begin with one of the biggest ministries and the mixing with the world, occult, New Age, humanism, and soulish realm. Let's examine Bethel Church – Pastor Bill Johnson of Redding California.

Bethel & New Age with Christalignment

Bethel has encouraged and endorsed many heretical things that I discovered in my research. One is their scandals is with a connection to a group called Christalignment. Due to the backlash of Christians, they have backed off…but still have things to do with them.

This group is trying to say that they are soul-winning at all these gay and New Age festivals, but I seriously doubt that is their motive. They are doing tattoos, reading palms, doing "Destiny Cards", etc. They are making a mockery of Jesus' name! Then they try to do healing (really, it's New Age healing – energy healing).

Let's just see what others say about this group:

According to TruNews, "Bethel Church, a California non-denominational charismatic megachurch, has aligned itself with a group that promotes what are essentially satanic tarot cards to perform readings on its members." (TruNews, 2017) In a related article post this one, the pastor who oversees the Creative Arts department for the Church and School of Supernatural Ministry is in this Christalignment group and defends her position in this demonic group. She proclaims, "We see many examples in Church history of creatively expressing the message of the Gospel through worldly, and even demonically inspired, expressions." (TruNews, 2017)

According to Bethel's own website where they are forced to defend their position on this group because of the obvious associations and answers from their staff, their response is, "The Hodges feel called to share the Gospel with a people group that most of us would feel unsure of how to approach. We value their efforts to minister to unbelievers in the ways they can more easily receive it and in the places they are going, like New Age festivals." (Bethel Church, 2018)

This answer is hardly a renouncing of the association with divination, which is abhorrently rejected by God. When you examine Christalignment's website it is obvious what they are doing. It's mixing divination with the gospel, which is forbidden to God. It's like calling something Christian Yoga. It's forbidden.

God cannot allow mixing with satanic things! According to their website, "Christalignment teams are trained in destiny reading, Presence therapy, trauma recovery, entity cleansing, relationship alignment and physical healing using divine energy. Dream interpretation is done using the Hebraic method which can facilitate deep spiritual alignment. Christalignment encounters coming from the third heaven realm bring lasting life transformation and guidance. The team are trained as intuitive readers and will address all client questions." (Christalignment, 2018)

As you explore their website you will notice the participation in drag queen festivals, sex, New Age, Queer, Mind Body & Spirit Expo, etc. They are so into the satanic that it's a shame that Bethel does not speak out against this atrocity, much less endorse it through their staff members, etc. They also have signs at their facilities that they give tattoos, readings, take people to the third heaven, etc. In other words, they do spirit travel and psychic things. This is satanic to the core.

Let's Look at the Eli Spirit of Many Churches. Many ministers put their children in charge of the ministry because they want to leave a legacy. However, many of the children are out of control with it. They will answer to God for this like Eli did. When the children don't respect the vision that God gave the founder, then it's off in error.

Also, many ministers will change their doctrine if their children get off in sin. For instance, if the child becomes a homosexual, they will begin accepting it in their church, etc. This is the spirit of Eli. We must love what God loves and hate what He hates.

Let's Look at Kenneth Copeland

Kenneth Copeland is very controversial due to his relationship with the Pope. It is obvious due to the meeting where the Pope sent his representative to Kenneth Copeland's meeting to come in UNITY with the faith stream of the church/Pentecostals.

Apparently, Kenneth Copeland partnered with the Pope (and even went to visit him with several evangelical ministers) and decided to partner the evangelicals in the ecumenical movement. I was shocked when I watched the video in which they did all of this. This website understands what is really happening, "Last night, October 24th, 2017 Kenneth Copeland held an ecumenical meeting in Kansas City Missouri with Pope Francis watching by video and his representatives present. In this video Copeland claims to be god's anointed prophet and claims to have the power of god to bring fire from heaven to 'burn the stubble', presenting a veiled threat to all the churches who do not get in step with the ecumenical movement." (AD Blog, 2017)

In addition, this website adds, "Kenneth Copeland leads the way for the anti-Protestant Reformation propaganda. That born-again believers should re-unite with the apostate Roman Catholic Church under Jesuit Pope Francis. They are staging a counterfeit 'New Apostolic Reformation' to destroy the true church." They are right on it!

You need to research him more. He has partnered with this apostasy. Check out **www.kairos2017.com**.

The New Apostolic Reformation is most definitely after the very fabric of the traditional church.

Let's Look at Bishop Carlton Pearson

This is a sad story. Bishop Pearson used to be a fundamentalist Pentecostal preacher on fire for God until he said God spoke to him that Hell doesn't exist, all people go to heaven, and has adopted the New Age religion. He was Oral Robert's spiritual son until this happened then he fell from grace.

Now he is a PEACE AGENT (I suspect for the Pope). He is always fighting against traditional preachers. You can see this on his Facebook page. Let's examine his website:

He labels himself as, "Progressive Spiritual Teacher, Thought Leader, Sacred Activist/Humanist, Peace Agent" (Pearson, 2018)

He advertises for the Expanding Consciousness Network, which is a coexist network. Remember how I said he fights against traditional Pentecostal preachers?

Right on his front page he has an advertisement, "Support the movement against extreme religious tyranny, unreasonable dogma, fear-based theologies, etc." Who do you think he's talking about? US. His ministry that has converted to completely New Age shows the rest of the church where they are all headed to by partnering with the Pope!

This ecumenical movement is blending for a new age religion. It's all working to coexist together.

They even made a movie about him called, "Come Sunday". They explain how he's prayed with presidents and how powerful he is in the Pentecostal world. (This is describing him in the beginning of the story). In the movie Bishop has a homosexual keyboard player who is dying of lymphoma (aids) and asks him if he is going to Hell for being gay. Bishop tells him Hell doesn't exists because Jesus loves everyone. How sad.

I pray people watching this movie knows the difference. The movie ends with him preaching in a gay church talking about being an outcast in society. He says that he does not like fear preaching. He now preaches regularly at All Souls Unitarian Church in Tulsa, Oklahoma. Now he is famous for preaching a message of inclusion (ecumenical). You can watch his movie on Netflix.

This is sadly what the ecumenical movement looks like:

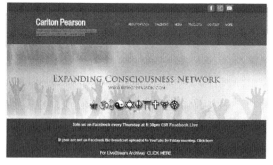

Let's Look at Oprah Winfrey

Oprah Winfrey is known as the New Age Queen. She has her own New Age network that promotes New Age ideology, and some say it's her church. I watched a YouTube video one time where Oprah says the reason she is not a Christian is because when she was a child she heard that God is "jealous" for us. She said that if that is the kind of God that he is to where he will get "jealous" of his own people, that she didn't want anything to do with him. "Oprah Winfrey reports that her impatience with 'rules, belief systems and doctrines' began when she, in her late 20s, heard a Baptist pastor say that God was jealous." (Coppenger, 2008)

She is famous for her television show she did for many years called Oprah - a talk show featuring people from all over the world, in which she pushed her New Age doctrine.

She often spoke against Christianity on the show. After retiring from the show (which was after Obama won presidency), she became more involved in politics.

She is a part of the ecumenical movement. She is now partnered with many key evangelists and featured on her television network.

When T.D. Jakes invited her to conduct her New Age classes in with his *Woman Thou Art Loosed* conferences, we knew he had flipped. Many in the church were astonished that he would do such a thing. Now his conferences look completely New Age.

The New York Times explains, "Yet the Church of Winfrey is at most partly Christian. Her show featured a wide, if drearily similar, cast of New Age gurus." (Oppenheimer, 2011) This article explains how she used her black church style to lure Americans into this new religion.

Now she's considering running for the presidency. She is New Age all the way and we should not trust her at all.

She has partnered with Tyler Perry who acts like Madea. Madea is a very funny character, but when it comes down to it, it is a man dressed as a woman. Ever since he partnered with Oprah he is very perverted and his movies too. It's very sad.

I just hate it that he's partnered with this New Age agenda. Bible says to touch not the unclean thing.

Let's Look at TD Jakes

As I pointed out earlier, T.D. Jakes invited Oprah to speak at his *Woman Thou Art Loosed* conference years ago and it ruined him spiritually. I've been in this vein for over 30 years and I've known his ministry a very long time. It was a shock to see that he was allowing this New Age teachings in his most famous conferences. Now his conferences just look New Age completely.

This event is called Mega Fest, so let's examine 2017's event:

Destiny World at TD Jakes' Church

This is the children's area. It looks like a warehouse with a circus area. It has inflatables, etc. "This summer experience the most magically interactive adventure on earth at the MegaKidz conference in Dallas, Texas! Thousands of kids from all over the world, including South America, China, and South Africa, are invited to "Experience the Adventure." Imagine a new world, where kids are encouraged to explore and play in an enchanting environment brimming with animated characters, engaging games, and more!

MegaKidz is the new world, and this exciting conference will inspire young hearts to believe in themselves through myriad adventure-themed interactive sessions, as well as age-appropriate live music performances and bounce-tastic games, among other experiences!" (MegaFest, 2018) Please notice the words "magically", "new world", and "enchanting". Does this not sound New Age to you or what? Pathetic! Then they have a child on the webpage with her hands over her eyes like the 666 symbol.

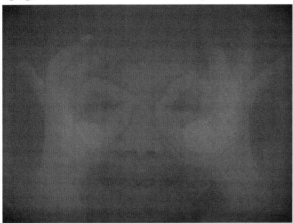

I just had to show you the picture to show you what I was talking about. How sad is this? This is an Illuminati signal.

It matches his logo though!

According to Dallas News, he conducts a talent contest for the youth which is designed for the "brothers and sisters of color to have a place to launch their idea." This is in the style of Shark Tank. They have a chance to, "Judges will pick a $15,000 prize winner for grades 6-8 and grades 9-12, and award four additional $5,000 runner-up prizes for other impressive ideas." (Dallas Morning News Editorial, 2017)

Look how he is described on his own website, "Bishop T.D. Jakes, one of the world's most revered masterminds, leverages his pioneering vision and instinct to serve others in areas extending beyond the church. In order to help lead people to their destiny, you have to meet people where they are in life." (T.D. Jakes, 2018)

He's also featuring his book tour of his new book *SOAR!* Which is about entrepreneurship. It's another self-help book.

Isn't it funny that Toyota is sponsoring it? This is suspicious period.

Another sponsor for this book tour is called The Dream Project. This is a project for black people through BET television and other sponsors.

When you click on their website, www.dreamprojectonline.com, it shows you more of their projects. One of those is called *Rolling Out*. When you click on that, it takes you to a black website focused on the who's who of black people and what is happening in entertainment, culture, music, videos, etc. They have a conference called *RIDE CONFERENCE.*

When you click on that it's another Pope initiative! It's called *Ride Conference* – Innovative Change Agents. Remember I told you that when you hear the word "agent" to think about the Pope and the one world religion. Agents I've discovered so far are:

Change Agents (leaders – movers/shakers)

Peace Agents (Coexist Leaders of religion)

Hope Agent

I'm sure there's many more.

Well guess who is sponsoring this *Ride Conference*? (You should always look at these things because this is where the money is). Southern Company (logo is a triangle), Microsoft (of course), McDonalds, Stanley and Toyota! (Ride Conference, 2018)

When you watch the video of this Ride Conference, the speakers are wearing all-seeing eye shirts, black and white, doing Satanic hand symbols, etc. It's all Illuminati! You've got to see it.

Let's Look at TBN

Law of Attraction - There is More to the Secret –

Quantum Physics.

This is on their website:

There is More to the Secret TV Show

Are these claims just wishful thinking? What vital information do Christians need to know about this world-wide phenomenon? re there biblical principles beyond the Law of Attraction that

Christians can use to effect change in the world around them? "There is More to the Secret" uncovers the answers with a sound, biblical foundation and a desire to discover the truth from the Bible and trusted Christian sources. Can Quantum Physics explain how the secret law of attraction works or does the Bible offer a better explanation? "The Secret" claims the universe can grant all your wishes. Could it be that the latest scientific findings on the origins of the universe point directly to the God of the Bible? Join us as we venture beyond the earth-bound philosophy of the law of attraction to reveal the Ultimate Power of the universe. There is More to the Secret will change your understanding of the immeasurable power of God ... forever! (TBN, 2018)

This show is based upon a blockbuster New Age movie called *The Secret*.

Here is a picture to show you what is on The Secret's website (www.thesecret.tv)

Here is the Show on TBN:

Same logo, with a little different font. However, it is the same source. It is pure divination and occult.

The New Age religion tells us to "look within" and this show's focus is on teaching people THE LAW OF ATTRACTION. Yes, I understand that as we think so we are, etc. I also understand that as we speak, so shall we have. However, when we get to the point that we control our mind to make things happen, that is divination! It's like sorcery. First of all, we do not make anything happen; God does. We believe his word yes. We trust in him yes. He is the one that makes it happen. If we take the glory, we are treading on dangerous territory! Where is faith in God anymore?

This generation wanting the MORE and going the extra-biblical route to get it is of the devil. Is the cross not good enough to be saved? They are seeking after the Tree of Knowledge of Good and Evil.

They are reaching after knowledge of things they should not. They want more, more, and more knowledge instead of just believing in the word of God. This is the same mistake that Eve made. "God knows that if I eat of this fruit that I will know MORE." This is basically what she was thinking. We know the price they paid as well. On Billy Graham's website he says, "Instead, Satan told them, if they ate it they would be transformed and become as powerful and as wise as God. What a temptation — to become like God!" (BGEA STAFF, 2013)

TBN's founder, Paul Crouch, was wearing the Catholic clothing for years before he passed. It always confounded me as to why he dressed like that. Then, when I discovered the ecumenical movement, then it made sense to me.

There are many questionable new shows on TBN.

Let's Look at Hillsong

This church has been doing so many things exposing their ecumenical and partnership with another Jesus. Recently they hosted an event called the *Alpha Conference*. This conference is sponsored by the Pope and is completely ecumenical.

This agenda is to start bible studies in all communities to spew their vomit into unsuspecting victims. Then, Hillsong participated in the sacraments with the monstrance and all.

Even on their website for the conference – www.alphausa.org, you will see the Catholic information. It's just plain ridiculous that we've gotten this far down the ecumenical path. However, it's not much of a shock when we consider the antics of Carl Lentz from their New York campus. This man has been on national TV and so politically correct when it comes to acceptance of homosexual lifestyle, tattoos, skinny jeans, etc.

According to the New York Times, he writes in his book, *Own the Moment*, "I have a real palpable disdain for religious jargon. I grew up in church. I ran from church." (Harris, 2017) As you can tell by his statement, it's feeding along the lines of the banter of anti-Christianity that has been going around. I've talked about these many times in these books.

They are turning people against Christianity and the "fundamentalist" or "old school Christianity". He obviously thinks he has a much better version of it. NOT.

Hillsong's New York church had a stripper at their Women's Conference. No lying! It is so worldly! "Today we cover two stories regarding Hillsong. First, Pastor Carl Lentz appearing with and praising Oprah Winfrey, telling Christians we should 'emulate her love of Jesus.' Never mind that Oprah's 'Jesus' is not the Son of God, but rather a 'good teacher.'

The second story today involves a Hillsong Youth leader appearing at a women's conference as 'the Naked Cowboy' along with Broadway dancers and yes, he appears to have no clothes on." (Stand Up for the Truth, 2016)

Need I say more?

Hillsong Music

Their music gets more bizarre as time goes by. They produced a video that was morbid. It is literally labeled as creepy on YouTube. Many videos mocking it. It's called *PEACE* video. It's obviously a picture of partnering with the Pope and the Great Whore of Babylon. "It is Satanic and not Christian. The Antichrist is going to come in the name of Peace (which is theme of this video). He is a counterfeit

Christ. The Antichrist is going to use our terms – Christian vernacular against the church.

He is going to twist the word and doctrine. (This woman is right on it!). She also explains how the Catholic Church is obvious but churches like IHOP, Bethel, Hillsong, and Morningstar Church – all these that are associated with the NAR movement. These are apostate churches as well and they are fooling the baby Christians who do not know their word." (Summers, 2018). This woman has a great sense of what is going on in the world and in the church!

Then Hillsong London did a literal Voodoo Dance Routine with the 2016 Easter special. Creepy. (Vigilant Christian, 2016)

On the stage they had people dressed up in voodoo outfits with creepy music playing like a tribal drum. Terrible.

Let's Look at IHOP

International House of Prayer is led by Pastor Mike Bickle. He hosts a yearly conference called *One Thing*. He has partnered with the Pope and I suspect it's been since the 70s.

Apparently, he was previously Catholic and still teaching Catholic practices such as contemplative prayer. Contemplative Prayer is a mystical practice and not godly. They try to say that they are being "quiet" before the Lord, but it is way more than that.

At his *One Thing* conference (which is week after Christmas), he hosts a Catholic One alongside called *The Catholic Track*. They have ecumenical dialogue with all the guests about Catholic beliefs and merging with Protestant beliefs. It is sad that they have partnered their anointed event with the Great Whore. The Catholic church is the head of the ecumenical movement and they want everything to lead back to Rome.

He no longer hosts this event every year. Many of the big ministries are now changing their structure, logos, responsibilities, etc. I believe it's because of this big RESET that's coming.

As you can see Bride, the battle is raging for your soul and your family. This is why judgment must come.

Apostasy + Idolatry = Judgment.

Bride, I've only pointed out a few ministries. There are many in the ecumenical movement. I pray you really research all of this.

6

God's Heart About Judgment – Biblical Overview

Most people do not believe anymore that God is a god of judgment. However, he very much is! From the beginning of time he judged! He is the holy judge! Sin has consequences!

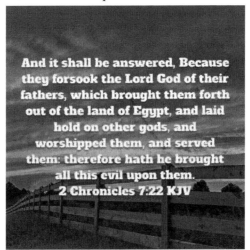

And it shall be answered, Because they forsook the Lord God of their fathers, which brought them forth out of the land of Egypt, and laid hold on other gods, and worshipped them, and served them: therefore hath he brought all this evil upon them.
2 Chronicles 7:22 KJV

Lucifer & Fall from Heaven

Let's start with this first judgment. Let's talk about Lucifer who is now Satan. Lucifer was God's best angel. He was highly favored. He was God's praise and worship leader. Well, he thought he was better than God, so he turned 1/3 of the angels against him. He caused a rebellion in Heaven (which is why we all came to Earth because God wanted our WILL to be tested before he let us in!)

> *Isaiah 14:12-17 - 12 How art thou fallen from heaven, O Lucifer, son of the morning! how art thou cut down to the ground, which didst weaken the nations! 13 For thou hast said in thine heart, I will ascend into heaven, I will exalt my throne above the stars of God: I will sit also upon the mount of the congregation, in the sides of the north: 14 I will ascend above the heights of the clouds; I will be like the most High. 15 Yet thou shalt be brought down to hell, to the sides of the pit. 16 They that see thee shall narrowly look upon thee, and consider thee, saying, Is this the man that made the earth to tremble, that did shake kingdoms; 17 That made the world as a wilderness, and destroyed the cities thereof; that opened not the house of his prisoners?*

He ended up kicking him out and now he tries to stop us from entering in where he can no longer go.

Actions that Brought Judgment	Turned God's angels
Judgment	Pride of Lucifer
Consequence:	Kicked out of Heaven Forever & In Hell

ADAM & EVE

Adam and Eve were God's first humans. God breathed into Adam and personally made him out of the dust of the Earth. It's really a very beautiful love story. Then, he saw that Adam was lonely and caused Adam to fall asleep and took a rib out of his side and created him a Woman to be by his side as a helpmeet.

God also created this beautiful garden for them to enjoy. He instructed them that they could enjoy everything in that garden except off one tree – the Tree of Knowledge of Good and Evil. He told him NOT TO EAT OFF THAT TREE OR HE WILL DIE.

So, here's Eve who listen to the snake (the devil) and she eats the fruit off the tree then convinces Adam to do the same. So, God is walking in the garden and asked them what happened and Adam blamed Eve, then Eve blamed the snake and they WERE ALL JUDGED.

Genesis 3:1-23 - 3 Now the serpent was more subtil than any beast of the field which the Lord God had made. And he said unto the woman, Yea, hath God said, Ye shall not eat of every tree of the garden? 2 And the woman said unto the serpent, We may eat of the fruit of the trees of the garden: 3 But of the fruit of the tree which is in the midst of the garden, God hath said, Ye shall not eat of it, neither shall ye touch it, lest ye die. 4 And the serpent said unto the woman, Ye shall not surely die: 5 For God doth know that in the day ye eat thereof, then your eyes shall be opened, and ye shall be as gods, knowing good and evil.

133

6 And when the woman saw that the tree was good for food, and that it was pleasant to the eyes, and a tree to be desired to make one wise, she took of the fruit thereof, and did eat, and gave also unto her husband with her; and he did eat. 7 And the eyes of them both were opened, and they knew that they were naked; and they sewed fig leaves together, and made themselves aprons. 8 And they heard the voice of the Lord God walking in the garden in the cool of the day: and Adam and his wife hid themselves from the presence of the Lord God amongst the trees of the garden. 9 And the Lord God called unto Adam, and said unto him, Where art thou? 10 And he said, I heard thy voice in the garden, and I was afraid, because I was naked; and I hid myself. 11 And he said, Who told thee that thou wast naked? Hast thou eaten of the tree, whereof I commanded thee that thou shouldest not eat? 12 And the man said, The woman whom thou gavest to be with me, she gave me of the tree, and I did eat. 13 And the Lord God said unto the woman, What is this that thou hast done? And the woman said, The serpent beguiled me, and I did eat. 14 And the Lord God said unto the serpent, Because thou hast done this, thou art cursed above all cattle, and above every beast of the field; upon thy belly shalt thou go, and dust shalt thou eat all the days of thy life: 15 And I will put enmity between thee and the woman, and between thy seed and her seed; it shall bruise thy head, and thou shalt bruise his heel.

16 Unto the woman he said, I will greatly multiply thy sorrow and thy conception; in sorrow thou shalt bring forth children; and thy desire shall be to thy husband, and he shall rule over thee. 17 And unto Adam he said, Because thou hast hearkened unto the voice of thy wife, and hast eaten of the tree, of which I commanded thee, saying, Thou shalt not eat of it: cursed is the ground for thy sake; in sorrow shalt thou eat of it all the days of thy life; 18 Thorns also and thistles shall it bring forth to thee; and thou shalt eat the herb of the field; 19 In the sweat of thy face shalt thou eat bread, till thou return unto the ground; for out of it wast thou taken: for dust thou art, and unto dust shalt thou return. 20 And Adam called his wife's name Eve; because she was the mother of all living. 21 Unto Adam also and to his wife did the Lord God make coats of skins, and clothed them. 22 And the Lord God said, Behold, the man is become as one of us, to know good and evil: and now, lest he put forth his hand, and take also of the tree of life, and eat, and live forever: 23 Therefore the Lord God sent him forth from the garden of Eden, to till the ground from whence he was taken.

Actions that Brought Judgment	Adam & Eve ate off the forbidden tree. Satan the serpent deceived them. Adam and Eve sought after too much knowledge.
Judgment	They were stripped of their rights in his kingdom because of their touching the "unclean thing".
Consequence	**Adam** – must work by the sweat of his brow now. Things are not easily handed over like they were. **Eve** – now has hard labor in childbirth. **Both** - They were kicked out of the garden. They no longer have access to the Tree of Life. The snake - had his legs removed and caused to slither and eat dust rest of his life. Satan was told that Jesus would stomp on his head one day.

NOAH

- God saw
- God judged
- God prepared his people. He prewarned Noah
- Revealed to Noah what the judgment will be & instructed him on what to do to get ready for the judgment
    - All during the preparations, God instructed Noah
    - He was with him the whole time
    - Noah went through great persecution from mankind. They thought he was crazy
- Noah obeyed God amidst all per persecution
- Judgment came – 40 days and 40 nights
    - Ch 7 vs 16 the Lord shut him in. This is key because I can't imagine what it must have sounded like when rain came for the first time like Noah said. Before this, water came up through the ground. Now people are outside the boat drowning and probably screaming wanting in the boat. God shut him in and protected his people.
- After 40 days and they came to land, restoration came

Genesis 6:1-22 - 1 And it came to pass, when men began to multiply on the face of the earth, and daughters were born unto them, 2 That the sons of God saw the daughters of men that they were fair; and they took them wives of all which they chose. 3 And the Lord said, My spirit shall not always strive with man, for that he also is flesh: yet his days shall be an hundred and twenty years. 4 There were giants in the earth in those days; and also after that, when the sons of God came in unto the daughters of men, and they bare children to them, the same became mighty men which were of old, men of renown. 5 And God saw that the wickedness of man was great in the earth, and that every imagination of the thoughts of his heart was only evil continually. 6 And it repented the Lord that he had made man on the earth, and it grieved him at his heart. 7 And the Lord said, I will destroy man whom I have created from the face of the earth; both man, and beast, and the creeping thing, and the fowls of the air; for it repenteth me that I have made them. 8 But Noah found grace in the eyes of the Lord. 9 These are the generations of Noah: Noah was a just man and perfect in his generations, and Noah walked with God. 10 And Noah begat three sons, Shem, Ham, and Japheth. 11 The earth also was corrupt before God, and the earth was filled with violence. 12 And God looked upon the earth, and, behold, it was corrupt; for all flesh had corrupted his way upon the earth.

13 And God said unto Noah, The end of all flesh is come before me; for the earth is filled with violence through them; and, behold, I will destroy them with the earth. 14 Make thee an ark of gopher wood; rooms shalt thou make in the ark, and shalt pitch it within and without with pitch. 15 And this is the fashion which thou shalt make it of: The length of the ark shall be three hundred cubits, the breadth of it fifty cubits, and the height of it thirty cubits. 16 A window shalt thou make to the ark, and in a cubit shalt thou finish it above; and the door of the ark shalt thou set in the side thereof; with lower, second, and third stories shalt thou make it. 17 And, behold, I, even I, do bring a flood of waters upon the earth, to destroy all flesh, wherein is the breath of life, from under heaven; and everything that is in the earth shall die. 18 But with thee will I establish my covenant; and thou shalt come into the ark, thou, and thy sons, and thy wife, and thy sons' wives with thee. 19 And of every living thing of all flesh, two of every sort shalt thou bring into the ark, to keep them alive with thee; they shall be male and female. 20 Of fowls after their kind, and of cattle after their kind, of every creeping thing of the earth after his kind, two of every sort shall come unto thee, to keep them alive. 21 And take thou unto thee of all food that is eaten, and thou shalt gather it to thee; and it shall be for food for thee, and for them. 22 Thus did Noah; according to all that God commanded him, so did he.

Actions that Brought Judgment	Earth filled with violence. Angels having sex with humans and creating giants
Judgment	God destroys the Earth and everything in it because evil in their thoughts continually.
Consequence:	Noah and his family had to start all over. The whole Earth was destroyed; all plants, animals, sea creatures, etc. They had to start all over.

Notice Bride how God revealed to Noah the plans, showed him HOW TO GO THROUGH to prepare for the judgment. Then God showed him HOW TO GO THROUGH THE JUDGMENT.

God protected him. I still cannot imagine what it must have been like to hear the suffering of the people outside the boat.

I can't imagine losing my friends, etc. See, we do not think about these things, but Noah was human like we are.

Also, what do you think about how Noah had to build an ark for something that had never happened before? Wow! He must have really been persecuted for that one! Then, to have all the animals, birds and creeping things come out of nowhere to the ark? That had to freak out the humans. Then, consider the giants! How God protected him from the giants that were on the Earth! It's an amazing story! We must remember how he warned him, walked him and instructed him during, and then carried him through to the end! God will do the same. Now let's consider another judgment.

SODOM & GOMORRAH

- God heard "cry of Sodom & Gomorrah"
- God judged situation & even came to see
- God trusted Abraham & told him he was about to judge this city.

- Abraham interceded for them and God allowed him. God told him he will not destroy it if there are 10 righteous.

- Abraham's nephew and family were there. Lot actually came there with a huge multitude of people.

- When angels came to pull Lot out of there, the men of the city tried to have sex with the angels. They were very violent and tried to break in Lot's house to take the men.
  - Lot was so embarrassed that they would act like that and tried to offer his virgin daughters. They only wanted the men (fresh meat!)
  - Angels saw how violent the men were and pulled Lot back in the house.
  - Angels blinded the men.

- Angels sat down with Lot and warned him. They told him that he must get his family out as soon as possible, that they were destroying the city.
  - Lot's sons laughed at him. Did not want to leave with him.

- God gave Lot time to save his family before he destroyed the city. The angels saw obviously that there was not even 10. So, God warned him and gave instructions on how to be saved.
  - Out of all the hundreds of thousands he brought there, all that left with him were his wife and two daughters! Then they didn't want to leave so the

angels had to drag them out!

- Angels warned Lot not to let anyone turn around to see the destruction! Lot's wife didn't listen and turned into a pillar of salt. This means she was too tainted in her heart.
  - After they escaped his two daughters had sex with him to have kids because of fear. This means that even his daughters were perverted.
    - Isn't it sad that out of the hundreds of thousands who followed him that he came out just him? Everything he touched when he partnered with this rotten vile city grabbed his family. He lost it all due to "pitching his tent towards Sodom".
- When Lot and family were leaving, God wanted them to go to this one city, but Lot wanted to go to another one. God honored him!
  - Angel told Lot that **they cannot destroy the city UNTIL they get him and his family out!** See how God tried to save HIS people? This is God's hand of protection!

- God judged the cities (more than those two) with hail fire and brimstone out of Heaven and destroyed them! God not only destroyed the inhabitants in those cities but destroyed everything on it. Think about it Bride. He destroyed the land, animals, buildings, etc. EVERYTHING paid the price for the filth on that land!
- God never restored this land!

Did you know that God judges land for the sins of mankind? Yes, he does! He will make land pay! This is why the land will sometimes SWALLOW up people because the land will get vengeance!

Genesis 19:1-29 - 1 And there came two angels to Sodom at even; and Lot sat in the gate of Sodom: and Lot seeing them rose up to meet them; and he bowed himself with his face toward the ground; 2 And he said, Behold now, my lords, turn in, I pray you, into your servant's house, and tarry all night, and wash your feet, and ye shall rise up early, and go on your ways. And they said, Nay; but we will abide in the street all night. 3 And he pressed upon them greatly; and they turned in unto him, and entered into his house; and he made them a feast, and did bake unleavened bread, and they did eat. 4 But before they lay down, the men of the city, even the men of Sodom, compassed the house round, both old and young, all the people from every quarter: 5 And they called unto Lot, and said unto him, Where are the men which came in to thee this night? bring them out unto us, that we may know them. 6 And Lot went out at the door unto them, and shut the door after him, 7 And said, I pray you, brethren, do not so wickedly. 8 Behold now, I have two daughters which have not known man; let me, I pray you, bring them out unto you, and do ye to them as is good in your eyes: only unto these men do nothing; for therefore came they under the shadow of my roof. 9 And they said, Stand back. And they said again, This one fellow came in to sojourn, and he will needs be a judge: now will we deal worse with thee, than with them. And they pressed sore upon the man, even Lot, and came near to break the door. 10 But the men put forth their hand, and pulled Lot into the house to them, and shut to the door. 11 And they smote the men that were at the door of the house with

*blindness, both small and great: so that they
wearied themselves to find the door.12 And the
men said unto Lot, Hast thou here any besides?
son in law, and thy sons, and thy daughters, and
whatsoever thou hast in the city, bring them out
of this place: 13 For we will destroy this place,
because the cry of them is waxen great before the
face of the Lord; and the Lord hath sent us to
destroy it. 14 And Lot went out, and spake unto
his sons in law, which married his daughters, and
said, Up, get you out of this place; for the Lord will
destroy this city. But he seemed as one that
mocked unto his sons in law. 15 And when the
morning arose, then the angels hastened Lot,
saying, Arise, take thy wife, and thy two daughters,
which are here; lest thou be consumed in the
iniquity of the city. 16 And while he lingered, the
men laid hold upon his hand, and upon the hand of
his wife, and upon the hand of his two daughters;
the Lord being merciful unto him: and they brought
him forth, and set him without the city. 17 And it
came to pass, when they had brought them forth
abroad, that he said, Escape for thy life; look not
behind thee, neither stay thou in all the plain;
escape to the mountain, lest thou be consumed. 18
And Lot said unto them, Oh, not so, my Lord: 19
Behold now, thy servant hath found grace in thy
sight, and thou hast magnified thy mercy, which
thou hast shewed unto me in saving my life; and I
cannot escape to the mountain, lest some evil take
me, and I die: 20 Behold now, this city is near to flee
unto, and it is a little one: Oh, let me escape thither,
(is it not a little one?) and my soul shall live. 21
And he said unto him, See, I have accepted thee*

concerning this thing also, that I will not overthrow this city, for the which thou hast spoken. 22 Haste thee, escape thither; for I cannot do anything till thou become thither. Therefore the name of the city was called Zoar. 23 The sun was risen upon the earth when Lot entered into Zoar. 24 Then the Lord rained upon Sodom and upon Gomorrah brimstone and fire from the Lord out of heaven; 25 And he overthrew those cities, and all the plain, and all the inhabitants of the cities, and that which grew upon the ground. 26 But his wife looked back from behind him, and she became a pillar of salt. 27 And Abraham gat up early in the morning to the place where he stood before the Lord: 28 And he looked toward Sodom and Gomorrah, and toward all the land of the plain, and beheld, and, lo, the smoke of the country went up as the smoke of a furnace. 29 And it came to pass, when God destroyed the cities of the plain, that God remembered Abraham, and sent Lot out of the midst of the overthrow, when he overthrew the cities in the which Lot dwelt.

Actions that Brought Judgment	Sins were grievous! Accusations from the enemy were horrendous! Homosexuality and all perversion. They also had no heart for the poor.
Judgment	God heard. Then he come to see. He destroyed everything on that land by raining hell fire and brimstone on it. Everything that sin touched was wiped out basically. Even Lot's family was tainted.
Consequence:	Lost everything and everything that it touched was destroyed off the planet! God basically vomited on these cities with hell, fire and brimstone.

MOSES & CHILDREN OF ISRAEL – EGYPT

- The king was worried about the prophecies of a deliverer and the amount of children of Israel being born. As a result, he sent an order out to the midwives to kill all the males at birth. The midwives honored God and not the king. (Ex 1:7)
  - ○ God turned around and blessed the midwives! (Ex 1:17, 20)
  - ○ He blessed them with houses (vs. 21)
- God saw, then heard the cries of his people due to their taskmasters
- God saved Moses since birth for this purpose
- God talked to Moses and shared his heart about what he was going to do to Israel
- Moses interceded for Israel many times
- God gave him instructions on how to do everything. God was with him. He did not have to do it alone.
- Since Moses feared his speaking abilities, God gave him Aaron to speak for him.
- Through all the plagues and things poured out during the judgment to the Egyptians, God always protected the Israelites.

- When spirit of death came through the land, God instructed the Israelites to put the blood of the lamb on the doorposts of their houses and it would pass over them. Can you imagine how hard it was to sit safe in the house and to hear the Egyptians screaming and crying over their sons dying? How terrible that must have been to hear the judgment of God upon those people.

- Were all the people in Egypt bad people and deserved all that wrath? NO. But, they had to experience the same as the king BECAUSE THEY WERE ATTACHED TO HIM. The ones who were SEPARATE were safe. Remember this.
  - When there was darkness in Egypt the children of Israel had light!
- You know the story of how God fed them in the wilderness, etc. I can't point out all the miracles because that would be a whole book!
- God brought them out!

Actions that Brought Judgment	Children of Israel crying to God about Egypt's treatment of them.
Judgment	God heard. God sent Moses & Aaron to warn Egypt.
Consequence:	God sent the death angel and returned to Pharoah what he did to God's people. God got revenge and destroyed his whole army. They experienced many plagues, etc.

ELI & HIS CHILDREN

The story of Eli is very sad. Eli had two boys that he raised up in the church. (I'm making this story short due to space). He raised them up spoiled. He did not discipline them. They grew up to be priests in the temple but would sleep (immoral) with the people and treated the house of God with disrespect. God ends up judging Eli because of how he did his children.

God sent him Samuel to raise and God gave the blessing over to Samuel. Samuel was given a dream to where he saw the downfall of Eli and his children. When Eli found out he received his fate. This is a sad story.

Actions that Brought Judgment	Eli's children were disrespectful to Eli, elders of the city and everyone. They plundered the house of God through immoral sex and defiling the communion. They were out of control. Eli didn't do anything to stop them.
Judgment	God woke up Samuel with a dream and told him what he was about to do to Eli. Eli inquired to Samuel and it was sad for Samuel to tell him.
Consequence:	They all lost their lives in the same day. They died by the sword. Sad.

Two other situations of judgments that I will not elaborate on is Jeremiah and Ezekiel. However, I do want you to know that they are very similar. God told those prophets the vile things the Children of Israel were doing. **Mainly they lied to the nation and prophesied falsely.** They worshipped idols and did not honor God. It is JUST LIKE AMERICA TODAY.

There are many other judgments, but you get the point. Here are a few points to know:

- Anything the sin has touched where it's not repented will be judged along with the main instigator.
- If you are attached to a false prophet and you're paying them money or sitting in a pew going along with his sin, then you are just as guilty.
  - Think of it like you're driving a getaway car for him. You're in the seat driving but you overlook his sin because you're comfortable in that seat. You are just as guilty in God's eyes.
- In judgment, there is no excuses. We must be real with God. We must look at ourselves while we're being judged and allow God to clean us up. He's revealed the nastiness in our own hearts. Why did we stay in that knowing it was wrong? Why did we support and help that?
- God has got to clean his Bride in order to use her. He can't

use tainted vessels. He must cleanse. Judgment is cleansing.

- Judgment is an act of love. It is his way of pulling his hand back and allowing you to see what you've done. It's allowing you to be SMACKED OUT OF YOUR STUPOR. It's a come to Jesus moment. It's a TOUGH LOVE move.

- Judgment is better on Earth when we have a choice to change and get it right than to die in our condition and be judged later after we've spent a few thousand years in Hell suffering over that stupor.

- Judgment brings the reality to life that your priorities in life have been in the wrong place. What is more important?

Scriptures About Judgment:

Leviticus 18:26 Ye shall therefore keep my statutes and my judgments, and shall not commit any of these abominations; neither any of your own nation, nor any stranger that sojourneth among you:

Leviticus 19:15 Ye shall do no unrighteousness in judgment: thou shalt not respect the person of the poor, nor honor the person of the mighty: but in righteousness shalt thou judge thy neighbour.

Leviticus 19:35 Ye shall do no unrighteousness in judgment, in meteyard, in weight, or in measure.

Leviticus 19:37 Therefore shall ye observe all my statutes, and all my judgments, and do them: I am the Lord.

Leviticus 20:22 Ye shall therefore keep all my statutes, and all my judgments, and do them: that the land, whither I bring you to dwell therein, spue you not out.

Leviticus 25:18 Wherefore ye shall do my statutes, and keep my judgments, and do them; and ye shall dwell in the land in safety.

Leviticus 26:15 And if ye shall despise my statutes, or if your soul abhor my judgments, so that ye will not do all my commandments, but that ye break my covenant:

Leviticus 26:43 The land also shall be left of them, and shall enjoy her sabbaths, while she lieth desolate without them: and they shall accept of the punishment of their iniquity: because, even because they despised my judgments, and because their soul abhorred my statutes.

Psalm 19:9 The fear of the Lord is clean, enduring forever: the judgments of the Lord are true and righteous altogether.

Psalm 25:9 The meek will he guide in judgment: and the meek will he teach his way.

Psalm 33:5 He loveth righteousness and judgment: the earth is full of the goodness of the Lord.

Psalm 35:23 Stir up thyself, and awake to my judgment, even unto my cause, my God and my Lord.

Psalm 36:6 Thy righteousness is like the great mountains; thy judgments are a great deep: O Lord, thou preservest man and beast.

Psalm 37:6 And he shall bring forth thy righteousness as the light, and thy judgment as the noonday.

Psalm 37:28 For the Lord loveth judgment, and forsaketh not his saints; they are preserved for ever: but the seed of the wicked shall be cut off.

Psalm 37:30 The mouth of the righteous speaketh wisdom, and his tongue talketh of judgment.

Psalm 72:1 Give the king thy judgments, O God, and thy righteousness unto the king's son.

Psalm 72:2 He shall judge thy people with righteousness, and thy poor with judgment.

Psalm 76:8 Thou didst cause judgment to be heard from heaven; the earth feared, and was still,

Psalm 76:9 When God arose to judgment, to save all the meek of the earth. Selah.

Remember Bride, judgment is God's mercy. He wants us to know that "He is the Lord". He is a jealous God. He will share us with no other. I know it sounds funny, but he is the one who created us. It's for a reason. This world we are in is a test. He does not want us to end up like Lucifer (Satan) and become prideful in all the blessings of Heaven. We will have books of our lives and we will always be able to remember what we went through. Our lives are literal books! Are you giving him the pen?

Another point is that judgment is for cleansing. Are we going to curse God during it or repent and turn? Many are not listening to God because of false prophecies. Same things happened in Jeremiah's and Ezekiel's day.

7

Prophetic Words About Coming Judgment

Many prophets are speaking today, but so are the false prophets. In today's circumstances a huge tsunami is on the horizon. The perfect storm is coming to our country. This is the judgment. I must give credit to a great revivalist in Florida, Toby Wentz – he was a guest on WATB Radio and pointed out this analogy about the tsunami. He said that when a tsunami is coming that the force of the waters is so great as they are coming in from afar that the shore will pull back and recede out in the ocean to reveal the bottom of the ocean. It is at this time that the filth, jewels, rocks and all sorts of things are exposed.

I noticed reading in Ezekiel Bible Study that right before judgment is a great exposure. Then reading in Jeremiah is the same. So, this analogy makes sense.

The Word God Gave Me on January 16, 2018

Ichabod is Coming

The Lord gave me a dream last night and presented a word to give to the Body of Christ today. I don't take this lightly what He's asking me to release, but I must obey. We are in a 40 Day time of prayer and consecration repenting on behalf of the church and the sins that we have committed against God. We are addressing our wrong doings to Him so that His mercies may roll down from Heaven. It's not that it will stop judgment, but we're praying for Him to have mercy upon us. In all rights, our nation deserves to be judged harshly, if for nothing else but how the church has done both God and our nation. We have caused the nation to become dependent upon the government for provision and help because we quit doing our job of loving our neighbors. We have sorely neglected our own people and caused many to die to suicides, drug overdoses, etc. We must get real with God and admit what we have done to the nation that HE has entrusted us with.

We are asking Him to have mercy upon us and help us to carry out the mandate that He meant for this nation. I believe the mandate it to evangelize the entire planet. God wants us to send out more missionaries than we ever have in history! He wants us to be a victorious Bride! Now on this 16th day of repentance the Lord gave me **this word for the Bride.**

THIS YEAR JUDGMENT IS COMING TO THE BRIDE IN AMERICA. JUDGMENT BEGINS AT THE HOUSE OF THE LORD. YOU HAVE NEGLECTED YOUR FIRST LOVE AND TURNED TOWARDS MANY LOVERS. MY EYES ARE NOW FIXED UPON YOUR SIN AND IT SHALL BE RETURNED UNTO YOU THE STENCH OF THIS SMELL.

THIS STENCH WILL EXPOSE YOUR OWN SINS TO THE PUBLIC. WHAT I HAVE HIDDEN AND ASKED YOU TIME AND TIME AGAIN TO REPENT OF WILL NOW BE EXPOSED PUBLICLY FOR THE WORLD TO SMELL YOUR STENCH.

MANY OF YOU HAVE RELEASED FALSE WORDS UNTO MY PEOPLE FOR SELFISH GAIN AND HAVE NOT REPENTED NOR RELENTED UPON THOSE WORDS. THE VERY STENCH THAT HAS BEEN RELEASED SHALL BRING A STENCH UPON YOU. AS OF THIS YEAR I WILL SEND AN ANGEL TO EARTH TO WRITE ICHABOD UPON MANY MINISTRIES AND CHURCHES THAT HAVE LIED TO MY PEOPLE AND FALSELY REPRESENTED MY NAME. YOU HAVE WAVED THE BANNER OF PRIDE AND MISJUSTICE TO MY PEOPLE WHO CAME TO YOU CRYING OUT FOR HELP AND YOU REJECTED THEIR CRIES. I WILL REJECT YOUR CRIES AS WELL WHEN YOU ARE EXPOSED. MANY OF YOU ARE SO FAR GONE FROM MY PRESENCE AND THE GLORY HAS ALREADY DEPARTED THAT YOU WILL NOT EVEN KNOW MY GLORY HAS LEFT.

MANY OF YOU HAVE PICKED FAMILY MEMBERS AND LOVED ONES OVER ME AND MY WORD. YOU HAVE COMMITTED THE SINS OF ELI AND PLACED THEM AT THE DOORPOSTS OF YOUR CHURCHES AND LIVES. YOU HAVE COMPROMISED AND THIS STENCH SHALL COME BACK UPON YOU. YOUR MANIFESTATIONS OF SIGNS HAVE NOT BEEN FROM ME AND YOU HAVE TAKEN THE GLORY UPON YOURSELVES. IT IS NOT UNTO YOU THAT THESE THINGS HAPPEN. WHEN MY TRUE MIRACLES HIT THE EARTH, I WILL RECEIVE ALL THE GLORY. I WILL NOT HAVE ANY OTHER LOVERS BEFORE ME.

WHEN YOU LOVE YOURSELF AND YOUR IMAGE MORE THAN ME, THEN YOUR IMAGE SHALL YOU PASS WITH.

YOU SHALL FACE YOUR IMAGE THROUGHOUT ETERNITY AND FOREVER WITHOUT MY IMAGE. I CREATED YOU IN MY IMAGE AND I AM THE ONLY ONE TO RECEIVE THE GLORY. MY PEOPLE HAVE MOVED FAR FROM ME AND HAVE NOT EVEN CONSIDERED MY WARNINGS BECAUSE THEY REFUSE TO HEAR TRUTH IN THIS HOUR. TRUTH IS ABOUT TO ROLL OVER THIS NATION LIKE A WET GLOVE. IT WILL BE SO HEAVY LIKE LIQUID RAIN, THAT MANY WILL NOT BE ABLE TO STAND UNDERNEATH IT.

THIS WEIGHTINESS OF TRUTH WILL STOMP OUT THE FALSE & IMPURITIES. THIS WILL SQUEEZE OUT THE INFIRMITIES OF THE CHURCH BECAUSE I WILL HAVE NO OTHER GODS BEFORE ME. I WILL HAVE NO OTHER IDOLS BEFORE ME. I AM HOLY. I AM THAT I AM.

YES, MY MERCY IS GREAT BUT TO THOSE WHO HAD NO MERCY UPON MY PEOPLE I SHALL HAVE NO MERCY. IF YOU HAVE BEEN ASHAMED TO SPEAK THE TRUTH, I SHALL BE ASHAMED OF YOU WHEN THIS JUDGMENT HITS. TIME HAS RUN OUT. REPENT NOW AND TURN!

WHEN I WRITE ICHABOD ON THE CHURCH/MINISTRY DOORS, I WILL PUT ANOTHER IN THAT I HAVE RAISED UP FOR SUCH A TIME AS THIS. THIS WILL BE THE ONES I'VE HAD HIDDEN WHO HAVE NOT BEEN ADVANCED YET. THESE ARE ONES WHO HAVE BEEN TESTED AND TRIED AND WHO WILL NOT TAKE THE GLORY. AS IN THE STORY OF ELI AND HIS CHILDREN WHEN THEY WERE SINNING AGAINST THE CHILDREN OF ISRAEL AND ELI KNEW ABOUT THEM HAVING SEX WITH MY PEOPLE; WHEN THE ARK OF GOD WAS TAKEN, THEY DIED. I WILL REMOVE THE VERY IDOLS YOU HAD IN BETWEEN ME AND YOU THIS YEAR.

YOU WILL KNOW THAT I WILL NOT HAVE THAT BETWEEN YOU AND ME.

REPENT AND TURN AS THE WORD **ICHABOD** IS TRAVELING THROUGH THE LAND THIS YEAR.

Ichabod
1 Samuel 4:21 -
The glory is departed...

1 Samuel 4:11-22 - 11 And the ark of God was taken; and the two sons of Eli, Hophni and Phinehas, were slain. 12 And there ran a man of Benjamin out of the army and came to Shiloh the same day with his clothes rent, and with earth upon his head. 13 And when he came, lo, Eli sat upon a seat by the wayside watching: for his heart trembled for the ark of God. And when the man came into the city, and told it, all the city cried out. 14 And when Eli heard the noise of the crying, he said, What meaneth the noise of this tumult? And the man came in hastily, and told Eli. 15 Now Eli was ninety and eight years old; and his eyes were dim, that he could not see. 16 And the man said unto Eli, I am he that came out of the army, and I fled to day out of the army. And he said, What is there done, my son? 17 And the messenger answered and said, Israel is fled before the Philistines, and there hath been also a great slaughter among the people, and thy two sons also, Hophni and Phinehas, are dead, and the ark of God is taken. 18 And it came to pass, when he made mention of the ark of God, that he fell from off the seat backward by the side of the gate, and his neck brake, and he died: for he was an old man, and heavy. And he had judged Israel forty years. 19 And his daughter in law, Phinehas' wife, was with child, near to be delivered: and when she heard the tidings that the ark of God was taken, and that her father in law and her husband were dead, she bowed herself and travailed; for her pains came upon her.

20 And about the time of her death the women that stood by her said unto her, Fear not; for thou hast born a son. But she answered not, neither did she regard it. 21 And she named the child Ichabod, saying, The glory is departed from Israel: because the ark of God was taken, and because of her father in law and her husband. 22 And she said, The glory is departed from Israel: for the ark of God is taken.

Exposure Coming to the Church

As you can tell by the word given that God is about to bring judgment to the church. It will begin through natural disasters and exposure of the false. I told people last year when the exposure came to the White House that the church is next. From the White House to the small house, etc. Here are scriptures about exposure:

Ephesians 5:11 And have no fellowship with the unfruitful works of darkness, but rather reprove them.

Romans 16:17-18 - Now I beseech you, brethren, mark them which cause divisions and offences contrary to the doctrine which ye have learned; and avoid them

Ephesians 5:11 - And have no fellowship with the unfruitful works of darkness, but rather reprove them.

Colossians 2:8 - Beware lest any man spoil you through philosophy and vain deceit, after the tradition of men, after the rudiments of the world, and not after Christ.

2 Corinthians 11:13-15 - For such are false apostles, deceitful workers, transforming themselves into the apostles of Christ

2 Timothy 4:3-4 - For the time will come when they will not endure sound doctrine; but after their own lusts shall they heap to themselves teachers, having itching ears

Galatians 1:6-9 - I marvel that ye are so soon removed from him that called you into the grace of Christ unto another gospel

1 John 4:1 - Beloved, believe not every spirit, but try the spirits whether they are of God: because many false prophets are gone out into the world.

Matthew 7:15 - Beware of false prophets, which come to you in sheep's clothing, but inwardly they are ravening wolves.

1 Timothy 5:20 - Them that sin rebuke before all, that others also may fear.

Jude 1:4 - For there are certain men crept in unawares, who were before of old ordained to this condemnation, ungodly men, turning the grace of our God into lasciviousness, and denying the only Lord God, and our Lord Jesus Christ.

Ephesians 5:6-13 - Let no man deceive you with vain words: for because of these things cometh the wrath of God upon the children of disobedience.

1 Timothy 4:1 - Now the Spirit speaketh expressly, that in the latter times some shall depart from the faith, giving heed to seducing spirits, and doctrines of devils;

1 Thessalonians 5:21 - Prove all things; hold fast that which is good.

2 John 1:10 - If there come any unto you, and bring not this doctrine, receive him not into [your] house, neither bid him God speed:

2 Peter 2:1 - But there were false prophets also among the people, even as there shall be false teachers among you, who privily shall bring in damnable heresies, even denying the Lord that bought them, and bring upon themselves swift destruction.

Acts 20:29 - For I know this, that after my departing shall grievous wolves enter in among you, not sparing the flock.

Matthew 7:15-20 - Beware of false prophets, which come to you in sheep's clothing, but inwardly they are ravening wolves.

2 Peter 2:3 - And through covetousness shall they with feigned words make merchandise of you: whose judgment now of a long time lingereth not, and their damnation slumbereth not.

2 John 1:7 - For many deceivers are entered into the world, who confess not that Jesus Christ is come in the flesh. This is a deceiver and an antichrist.

Matthew 7:21-23 - Not everyone that saith unto me, Lord, Lord, shall enter into the kingdom of heaven; but he that doeth the will of my Father which is in heaven

When I went to Washington D.C. in March 2018, the Lord gave me a dream of a word to speak over the Supreme Court on our way out back to Tennessee.

On March 4, 2018

The Lord told me in a dream that I am to take a bible and stand to decree and prophecy on the top of the steps at the Supreme Court;

- That God's word is the truth and nothing but the truth!
- That truth will reign supreme in this country
- For God to expose the false and to reveal the heavy weight of truth to the nation

- That God's people will be hungry for truth
- For God to release His hidden ones to begin declaring truth from the mountaintops
- We partner with Heaven today that the will of the living God will be accomplished in the Earth. This means the God of Abraham, Isaac and Jacob!
- That God's justice of Truth will fall down like liquid rain
- That God would baptize His servants in the fire of truth!
- That God will open up media to speak truth! Bless them with best equipment and resources to educate the Bride
- The truth will be revealed concerning our president to the world
- We are to go to those other places first in the end up at the Supreme Court then go the top of the Supreme Court with the Bible and handed truth will roll over the nation with justice and judgment cleansing the house of God and preparing the bride for the return of Jesus Christ
- This officially ends and seals the 40-day prayer mission and repentance before God on behalf of the church and the nation. Let God's will be done

To the BOC;

Warning! Warning! Sirens are sounding! Jesus is coming soon, and judgment will begin in this nation of cleansing the church from the mega to the minor; from the White House to the small house. Get your houses in order. God is a God of holiness and purity.

Prepare ye the way of the Lord. The God of Abraham Isaac and Jacob will reveal himself to the church and expose the mockery of Jesus name. Exposure will begin.

It Has Begun

On May 30, 2018, we had on ABC's World News Tonight with David Muir an expose of Jesse Duplantis' plea to the church about a 54-million-dollar jet. He told the church that if Jesus was living today he would not be riding on a donkey. He would be on a jet. Of course, ABC News twisted the truth and only showed snippets of truth. Thus, they were talking about people's reactions on Facebook calling him a "hypocrite", etc. I believe this is just the beginning. It doesn't help that false preachers have misused prosperity gospel and mishandled God's word.

It's not that I'm against prosperity, it's when they go to the extreme with it.

Media will begin to lie more and come after the church. We must be able to discern what is truth and lies. They will begin to turn the people against fundamentalist Christians, so they will paint a bad light on us.

However, much truth will be in what they are exposing so we will see more. Just telling ya Bride. Also. If you are attached to hypocrisy, then when it is judged…so will you be judged because you are attached to that sin.

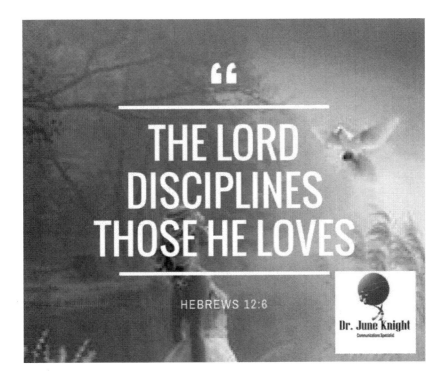

DREAM ABOUT EARTHQUAKE ON NEW MADRID
FAULTLINE IN CLARKSVILLE, TENNESSEE

In 2001 I recently moved to Clarksville, TN and the Cumberland River ran through it. This river is one of the outlets of Mississippi. I had a daughter in the 5th grade, and she was going to a school in downtown Clarksville. I did not know much about Clarksville when I had this dream:

I felt the Earth shaking so violently that it was bouncing me out of the bed. I knew it was an earthquake. I looked over the mountain to downtown Clarksville. (In Clarksville the downtown area is separated by a river). So, I was looking from one side of the river to downtown buildings. I could see the buildings at the top of the hill shaking violently.

I saw the buildings sink straight down into the ground like the ground had just swallowed them up. The whole downtown collapsed like one big sinkhole! It was utter destruction! I saw buildings on the side of the river literally fall over into the river! It was like that whole downtown area just collapsed and disappeared!

When I woke up, I was so shook up that I took my daughter to school that day and withdrew her from school! I home-schooled her due to the fear of this dream!

Since the dream I found out that most of Clarksville, TN is built upon one big sinkhole. I also found out that the New Madrid Faultline was that river going beside Clarksville! So, years later I went to school at Austin Peay State University which is right at the top of downtown. I always wondered if the earthquake would happen each day. It never did and then…

I remembered this dream when I hear all these prophecies lately, and I thought, "It's coming…it's coming." Get ready bride!

DREAM ABOUT MARTIAL LAW COMING
(written in my Clarion Call to UNITY book)

Most people with whom I talked throughout the nation believe they are preparing for future martial law.

I met people in Mississippi, Louisiana, Texas, Alabama, Florida, Ohio, Kentucky, Michigan, Indiana, and Arkansas who are all preparing for it. It boils down to this: The conservatives believe all this is coming, and the liberals believe we conservatives are all crazy. The day after I received that call from my spiritual father about Jade Helm, I was in Indiana visiting family at the family restaurant, and I told them, "My phone is not working, and neither is the data." They informed me that the communications had been down all morning.

166

I thought that was weird considering the lights were still on. I tell you that for four hours the cell phones, internet, cable, landline phones, etc. were all out. Afterwards, I informed my spiritual father what happened, and we both feel it was part of the Jade Helm exercises to see what happens when communications go down. It was very eerie. Six months later, I had a dream about martial law.

Here is the dream:

Dream about Martial Law

I was leaving a church with revival fires burning, and I was in my car in the parking lot. I was just about to put the car in reverse when all of a sudden, 10 big Army trucks carrying heavy equipment pulled up.

(In my dreams, I have these knowings - meaning I just know things/facts in the dream. I knew there was guillotines. I knew they were here to kill the Christians.)

I looked on the back of the trucks and saw equipment that looked like the folding tables we have at church. It looked like six-foot long tables but twice as thick. I knew they were portable coffins. When the men got out of the trucks, they were so full of evil, unlike anything I'd ever seen before. They were demonic, and they were on a mission to kill us. Their eyes looked black and hollow.

In my car, I started screaming, "Forget all the fluff in my ministry (meaning the highlighting ministries, interviews, etc.). I need to warn the Christians and tell them that these terrorists cannot kill us without God granting them permission! We don't need to fear! We have God on our side! We need to get in UNITY and reap the harvest! WARN THE CHRISTIANS!" Then, I woke up.

I encourage you to research on YouTube all the dreams the Lord is giving His people about martial law, etc.

Also, I encourage you to read my next book, *The Last American Bride*. I talk about drones and different things the government is doing to prepare for the mark of the beast.

Famine Coming

(written in my Clarion Call to UNITY book in 2016)

The Lord has spoken to me while writing this book that famine is coming to the world. As I have alluded to previously, God gave me a dream in 2013 of Obama on the Olympic Stands talking out of both sides of his mouth to Russia and U.S.A. We are headed into famine, sword and pestilence. See pic to the left:

So many Christian leaders are not talking about this right now. I hear a whole lot about revival and awakening coming, but they are not telling you that it is going to come through suffering.

+

It is going to come through trials and tribulation. We are headed into an economic collapse and the Bride is not ready. This book is attempting to help the Bride to be ready for the suffering ahead. During this famine, God will take care of us. We do not need to fear, but trust in the Lord.

When I traveled the United States in 2015, people from all the states are preparing. They are stocking food, etc., preparing for martial law and famine. God is warning his people. Listen to God in the Garden of the secret place.

KENT CHRISTMAS WORD 2018

Kent Christmas is a minister in Nashville, Tennessee and he gave a word to the church the end of December and it has spread like wildfire. I asked his office for permission to insert that word, however they turned it down since he is writing his own book around that word.

However, I can tell you some highlights of what I remember from that word:

- Judgment will begin in 2018 to house of God
- God is tired of the sports industry mocking God and they will be bankrupt due to this.
- Hollywood will be judged harshly
- False prophets will either die suddenly or face harsh judgment openly for lying to God's people, etc.

I can't remember all of it, but you can see all of it here: https://www.youtube.com/watch?v=5Raz0F0zuO0

Here is one mighty quote from the sermon, ""For Christians who no longer value My presence anymore and are lukewarm and My house has not been a priority in your lives, I'm going to withdraw from you this coming year" says God.

169

"I have blessed the lukewarm hoping that My blessings would make you love Me more and want to spend time with Me, but you have fallen in love with My blessings instead of Me. I am now going to remove My protection that I have had in your lives and in your house and over your families" says the Lord. "And when you cry out to Me, I will not answer you in that day." (Christmas, 2018)

Other ministers I encourage you to follow is:

- Jeff Byerly – Holy Spirit Wind
- Celeste Solum – Ex FEMA employee

WORDS BY JEFF BYERLY
(Given with Permission)
www.holyspiritwind.net
About Jeff:

The Lord is taking me out of my comfort zone once again! I have been blogging since December 2015 on https://holyspiritwind.net/ but now, as of 6-17-19, I will be reading messages that I have been given from the Lord on YouTube...I have no idea if I will get through all of them. My opinion about this is that things will be changing very quickly in the coming days and the Lord wants to get his message out to as many as possible. So by reading them on YouTube I will be touching a different audience. I pray that all of you are blessed by the things that I read but I also pray that the Lord would wake you up to the time that we are in so that you can get ready for his second coming. Blessings love and peace in the name of Yahshua ha Mashiach, Jesus Christ.

His servant Jeff Byerly
3-4-16
To My Bride:
Judgment is Set!

Do not be in awe and wonder about the impending doom, be in awe and wonder of your God.

Let the love that I have put in your heart be what comes out of your mouth.

DO NOT say "I told you so" DO NOT speak to people with a condescending, self-righteous, religious attitude I HATE THAT ! Show My love and show much compassion. This is your time to shine My bride, this is why you were born for such a time as this.

I take no pleasure in the destruction of the wicked, but I alone know the hardened hearts that will not turn to Me no matter what I do. I alone know if a man will turn to Me in repentance. I AM their maker and I AM their judge. If there was another way, I would choose it.

My judgments are righteous and final no man can question what I do. I AM a God of love and mercy. I AM longsuffering, patient, meek and humble, but I hate sin!

I cannot and will not stand aside and let evil deeds go unpunished.

I AM a holy God. If you knew the entirety of the sins of this nation (America) and the world, you would not be able to stand it, it would consume you and ruin you completely.

Yet I see these things endlessly, every day, every hour, every minute, every second.

The towers falling, was a warning to America, but not many have repented. Now an event will happen that will be many times greater in magnitude.

It will be devastating!

My warnings to the sinners are not being heeded and will soon STOP.

They only mock and scoff and ridicule and say "Where is your God!" they heap even more of My judgment on their own heads. Only My bride is heeding My warnings, very few are listening at all.

The judgments that come first are the things that I allow the enemy to do. You will see Satan's wrath because his time is short. Many of My own will be taken home to be with Me because of because of these horrific events that are going to take place. **You cannot pray these events away.** *Instead pray and intercede for the lost and hard in heart that they will humble themselves and come to Me with all of their heart.* That is what I require!

I have made the provision for the salvation of All that will call upon My name.

Weep ,Wail and Travail for the lost that will meet their end. Humble yourselves in intercession, call for a solemn assembly and fall on your faces before Me. **Thousands will arrive in hell because of the next event. IT IS SET!**

Do not be confused My beloved bride. This is not My wrath yet! **For you will NOT see My wrath.**

These things will Not even compare to My wrath. *Satan has very little power compared to Me and he can only do what I allow.* **My wrath is unbearable and no man or angel or any created thing can withstand it.** My wrath is borne out in "The Destroyer".

You cannot imagine the destruction that will occur. **The judgments will happen in rapid fire succession until the end, once they start**.

But behold I will make all things new, because that is what I do! This will not be the first time the earth will be suffering this destruction, but it will be the worst it has ever seen. As it was in the days of Noah so shall it be at the time of the coming of My Son.

WE ARE ONE!

Pray in the Spirit always and do not stop. These prayers are more powerful than you even know, and they are My perfect will. **I cannot wait to be with you forever, and there will be no veil, it will be removed; and you will see Me in all of My glory.** I have chosen every one of you and I will not lose any that The Father has given Me.

Just a little while longer My beloved, but first your transformation to bright, sparkling pure white!

I LOVE YOU MY BRIDE!

I Will Break Your Hardened Hearts
with My Hammer of Judgment
3-29 through 4-1-17

O wealthy, proud nations of the world you think you have no need of Me, for you have everything you need. You are rich in worldly things but spiritually you are wretched, miserable, poor, blind, and naked. **Your wealth is in this world, which is perishing, it will all burn!** *I counsel you to buy from Me gold refined in the fire, that you may be rich; and white garments, that you may be clothed, that the shame of your nakedness may not be revealed; and anoint your eyes with eye salve, that you may see.*

I came to you in your prosperity and you received me not. I came to those in third world countries and they received Me with great joy.

I AM pouring out My Spirit upon the meek, the humble, the poor, the contrite, downcast and downtrodden and they are overflowing with My Spirit. They are experiencing My glorious end time miracles already! **The third world countries who have no worldly wealth are becoming rich in Me.**

O civilized, westernized nations of the world, My end time flood of former and later rain will come to you when you have been made a third world country! Tribulation will come upon the whole earth. I told you that it would come even from the time of My earthly physical ministry. Nothing has changed, it cannot, for it is written. I said in this world you WILL have tribulation but be of good cheer for I have overcome the world. I have not changed My mind. **There are many false teachers and preachers in this day that will tell you this is not true and they are liars.** They only say good things that make your ears tingle with joy, but it is not the truth.

The fires of tribulation and persecution will refine you and the dross will float to the top and it will be skimmed out of you by Me.

I will humble the prideful and lofty ones. **I will bring down the ones that sit up high and think they cannot fall.** I say, repent! Cry, weep and wail on your faces before me with fasting before the LORD your God. **I long for you to say as David did, "My flesh trembles for fear of You, And I am afraid of Your judgments."** *Is not the fear of the Lord the beginning of wisdom?* **Yet you have become fools because you don't fear Me.**

I will break your hardened hearts with My hammer of judgment. **As many as I love, I rebuke and chasten.**

Those who have no chance to repent, I use as instruments of My wrath, that shall be poured out on the unrighteous as a last chance for repentance by My mercy and grace. I can take your heart of stone and give you a heart of flesh and though your sin be as scarlet, **I will make them whiter than snow.** *Place the blood of the Lamb upon the lintel and doorposts of your heart with hyssop, so that the **destroyer will pass over you.***

To My virgins **keep your lamp filled daily and stay awake, for seducing spirits have been loosed.**

Those who have let your oil get low, buy from Me pure oil so that the wicks of your lamps do not grow hard from impurities. The wick of your lamp is your heart. If the oil in your lamp is impure you will have to trim your wick and rid yourself of the hardness; these are the cares and desires of this world.

Those that still have a coal or ember left of My fire left within them need only for My Holy Spirit to blow His mighty wind to kindle a bright burning flame inside you again.

Stop blocking and let Him blow!

To those who have let your fire go out: I will relight your spirit and you will see that which has made your flame go out.

To those have never had My fire inside you: Let My all-consuming fire light a fire inside of you that you cannot contain!

I am coming at an hour that you do not think, so be at the ready!

If any man thinks he has figured out when My return is, and stays in in his sin thinking that I will not return for years and years; I will come when he is not ready and he will be put to shame.

175

This man will be cast into great tribulation and into the outer darkness where there will be weeping and gnashing of teeth. **All that love darkness will experience great pain when the light of My glory comes!**

I will destroy the darkness with the brightness of My coming!

Thank you Lord for your warnings that you give out of your mercy, grace and love, Jeffrey D. Byerly

---

The Shaking of My House Has Begun
Received 4-8 through 4-11-20
1 Peter 4:17-18 (AMPC)

For the time [has arrived] for judgment to begin with the household of God; and if it begins with us, what will [be] the end of those who do not respect or believe or obey the good news (the Gospel) of God? And if the righteous are barely saved, what will become of the godless and wicked?

Hebrews 12:25-29 (AMPC)

So see to it that you do not reject Him or refuse to listen to and heed Him Who is speaking [to you now]. For if they [the Israelites] did not escape when they refused to listen and heed Him Who warned and divinely instructed them [here] on earth [revealing with heavenly warnings His will], **how much less shall we escape if we reject and turn our backs on Him Who cautions and admonishes [us] from heaven?** Then [at Mount Sinai] His voice shook the earth, but now He has given a promise: Yet once more I will shake and make tremble not only the earth but also the [starry] heavens.

Now this expression, Yet once more, indicates the final removal and transformation of all [that can be] shaken—that is, of that which has been created—in order that what cannot be shaken may remain and continue. Let us therefore, receiving a kingdom that is firm and stable and cannot be shaken, offer to God pleasing service and acceptable worship, with modesty and pious care and godly fear and awe; For our God [is indeed] an [all] consuming fire.

I speak now to My temples, you are those that I indwell, you are those that have let Me in to eat and fellowship with. A short time ago I told you to get your affairs in order but now I tell you, **the shaking of My house has begun.** *I have allowed for this relatively gentle shaking to awaken those that have been slumbering.* **Yes, this man-made pestilence has been allowed to begin to change completely the world as you know it.** Many of you know that things are not as the governments and media outlets are portraying them. **They are using this to forward their New World Order, which is the one world beast system.** *"Going to Church" as you have known it is a thing of the past.* **Very soon the only "church gatherings" that will be allowed by the government will be the ones that they run and** *you will need their mark to attend them.*

Of course, this will not be My church!

The biggest reason I have allowed this shaking is so that you who I indwell realize that **YOU ARE THE CHURCH**! Buildings mean nothing to Me! Programs mean nothing to Me!

Polished music means nothing to Me! Pre-planned sermons mean nothing to Me! Your tithing means nothing to Me, **give to the poor not the rich! Light shows, theatrics and what is called "prophetic arts" mean nothing to Me!** All these things glorify the flesh, I detest them! **COME, SEEK ME NOW IN YOUR PRAYER CLOSET, YOUR INNER CHAMBER. LOCK THE DOOR AND DO NOT COME OUT UNTIL YOU HAVE HEARD FROM ME. YOU MUST SEEK ME YOURSELF!**

This shaking will not stop but continue until the end of this age and **it will intensify** and become very violent, shaking both heaven and earth. **This shaking is to rid My house of the enticements, entrapments, bondages and idols of this world.**

If you ask Me, I will pick you out of the muck and mire that many have fallen in. **I will clean you off with My shed blood and with the washing of the water of My word, when you make the decision to repent before Me.** I will transform and renew your mind if you let Me. Just make the choice to not conform to the pattern and systems of this world and ask Me for the power to overcome continuously and never stop conversing with Me. I will place your feet upon The Rock that cannot be shaken, which is I, **but you must forsake the things of this world.** This shaking has come so that you know that the time is upon you. **It is by My mercy, love and grace that this has come.** *Yes, this judgment has been allowed by Me for the glory of My kingdom.* **Now rid yourselves of all filthy deeds of the flesh and the spirit!**

Some of you are asking, "What are these things that we must be rid of?" I will mention just 3 here. First and foremost, I see **spiritual pride.**

Most think that they are "good enough" but I say there is none good, no not one! A lot of you think that you have "arrived" and that you will not see tribulation but that number is very few and even these will see the reward of the wicked with their eyes but I will protect My witnesses. Did this not happen with the plagues of Egypt? My people saw the plagues, but they did not affect them. **Did not My people have light in their dwellings during the thick darkness?** *Did not the death angel passover when he saw the blood on the doorways of their abodes?* **My blood must be upon the doorposts and lintels of the hearts of those that are My houses.** You must be holy as I am holy and it is not of yourself, it is by My grace. **I say repent, humble yourselves before Me, ask for forgiveness, turn from your wicked ways and empty yourselves of everything of this world so that I may completely infill you and submerse you in My Holy Spirit.** You must do this continuously, not just once in a while and you must truly mean it **with all of your heart.**

Secondly, **the love of money, prosperity and the things of this world have taken too high a place in My houses.** Does it not say in My word that "the love of money is a root of all kinds of evil, for which some have strayed from the faith in their greediness, and pierced themselves through with many sorrows"? (1 Tim. 6:10) **Why is it that "so called" ministers of My word have private jets (and one isn't even good enough), expensive new mansions, multiple new vehicles, designer clothes, every new gadget and trinket that there is but** *I had no place to lay My head and didn't even know where My next meal would come from, when I walked as a son of man upon the earth?* Why do some that have plenty not share with those in need of daily sustenance?

179

This is especially true in America and the western nations, but it is coming to an end. Your money will soon be worthless after the fiery kick-off event. **This is when you will not buy or sell unless you take the mark of the beast and worship him. I mark My own and he marks his own.**

Thirdly, most who call themselves by My name, **look to the man Donald Trump more than Me to protect them.** They say that **He is the one who I had placed into the office and this is true but it was to test the hearts of the people.** He is an idol to many, but I am taking down **that idol from his high place.** You can see it now where before it was hidden, the presidential seal has been removed from his speaking podium. **But the reality is that he has not had the power that most thought he had for a while now.** The **real leader of America** has not gone away, and he will re-emerge from the shadows back into the spotlight and back to rule. (You can read this HERE in a message from 2018). **Donald Trump has been completely controlled by him since April of 2018.** (You can read this HERE in a message from 2019)

He is allowed to have a figurehead position for now, to control the people by giving them false hope, but soon he will be taken away completely in the fiery kick-off event in New York City. I have spoken of this many times but now more will believe what I have said is the truth.

My beloved, **I WANT ALL OF YOUR HEARTS AND I WANT YOU TO REACH THE HEARTS OF THE LOST IN MY POWER!**

The great anointing and the transformation will come to those who are ready.

Now is the end of time to be ready! **When you see the chaos and destruction brought forth by the fiery kickoff event it will be too late to prepare! You must do it now!**

PREPARE THE WAY FOR ME! HEED MY WORDS! EL ELYON - YAHUSHUA HA MASHIACH - JESUS THE CHRIST

As the Lord began to give me this message on 4-8-20 he put this old song into my head that I have not heard in quite a while.

Shakin' The House by Petra
There's a rumble in the distance
A trembling in the air
It's uncertain in direction
Does it come from here or there
It's approaching by the minute
Does it lead you to despair
Feel it shakin' your foundation
When you haven't got a prayer
Everything that can be shaken will be shakin' from within
Better have your house in order when the shakin' begins
Shakin' the house, shakin', shakin' the house, shakin'
Shakin' the house, shakin', shakin' the house, shakin'
Shakin', shakin' the house
You examine your foundation
Does it stand on rock or sand
When the smoke clears, does it bring fears
When houses fall or stand
In the fire of refining
With flames too high to douse
You remember someone saying
It's beginning in the house
Everything that can be shaken will be shakin'…

You Must Not Fear the "Coronavirus" or any Other Plague that Will Come.
2-1-20

At the end of the video that I did last week I mentioned that I heard from the Holy Spirit while praying about the "coronavirus", the first line from the old 70s song from **The Carpenters – We've Only Just Begun**. This was actually a confirmation from Him of a question that I asked earlier that week (the week of Jan 20, 2020). At that time I asked the Holy Spirit a question, basically "Is this "coronavirus" the global pandemic from the 4th seal?" His answer was **No** but He did elaborate, the things that He has warned about through His various voices, including myself, are starting to take place but **that events will become much worse than we are seeing even now.** *He also said that the "coronavirus" was not from Him,* **it has been concocted in a lab by men.**

This will kill many people, but **it will have nowhere near the size and effect that they will release during the 4th seal.** This "coronavirus" is a "test run" so that they can see exactly how people will react and to **perfect their methods of controlling the masses.** He also told me that **if we are living and praying Psalm 91 this plague and any others** *will not have any effect* **on His people.** (Psalm 91 is shown below)

The Holy Spirit has been speaking to me all week and this is what the Lord has told me to write to those who will listen.

"Listen to Me My children. There is so much happening in your world right now, so much confusion that the enemy is bringing upon the earth. **This is his plan and I am allowing it to try the hearts of men, even My precious elect-remnant-bride that I love so dearly.** You must be living *in the secret place* of the Most High and be abiding under the shadow of the Almighty.

You have My promises of protection in My word, but you must be obedient to what it says. Stay close to Me now! **You must not fear the "coronavirus" or any other plague that will come.** These are brought about by the evil men that worship your enemy. **Soon will come a plague that will dwarf the size and effect of this "coronavirus".** I have said that I will protect the place that you live in **if you are in Our secret place**, having an intimate relationship with Me.

Just repeating the scriptures with your lips does no good whatsoever, it must be your life!

I know that most of you did not think that you would see a time such as this upon the earth, but I tell you truly; you were born for such a time as this. I tell you that many more people are praying to Me now since the "coronavirus" has emerged and this is good! **Many will turn to Me as the judgments roll out upon this earth.** The divine purpose for you being here during this time upon the earth is to seek and save My lost sheep. This is the work that was prepared beforehand, even before there was time, for My elect-remnant-bride to do. *It is the great harvest that is reaped at the end of this age.*

So many have been deceived into thinking that they will escape at any moment, but it is not the truth.

Most of My elect-remnant-bride will not even listen to Me when I try to tell them this lovingly and gently because of **demonically inspired man-made doctrines** that have spread throughout the churches. There are events that have been written in the scriptures from My prophets of old that have to take place first. There are also events that have to take place that I have shown to My modern-day prophets, seers, watchmen and handmaidens as well. **For most, there will be a rude awakening when the fiery kickoff event happens, and they are still on the earth.** This is still coming, it is not delayed, My time is not yours and all of the events that I have told you that would precede this are coming as well.

After these events take place My warnings

to My people will stop completely.

Then **a more powerful anointing will fall upon those that have readied themselves as I have commanded, with their garments washed gloriously white by the water of the Word, without spot or wrinkle or any such thing.** (Eph 5:25-27) This is he who **has clean hands and a pure heart,** who has not lifted himself up to falsehood or to what is false, nor sworn deceitfully. He shall receive blessing from the Lord and righteousness from the God of his salvation. (Psalm 24:4-5)

I say this to you all, keep My command to persevere, I also will keep you from the hour of trial which shall come upon the whole world, to test those who dwell on the earth. (Rev 3:10)

If you did not have any trials or tribulations in this world, why would I tell you to persevere? **My people will not experience My wrath, but you will have trials and tribulations in this world. I use the enemy to refine you like fine silver and gold, so I can see Myself in you.** But be of good cheer because I have overcome the world and by My Spirit - you will overcome as well. **There may be pain in the night, but joy comes in the morning! I AM the bright and morning star!**

DO NOT GIVE UP! Overcome this world just as I did, by the Holy Spirit that lives in you because of My blood and you have My testimony and **you will even hate the life you have upon this earth when compared to the glorious life that lies ahead of you.** But before that, I am doing a work in your days that you would not believe it even if you were told! (Hab.1:5) It will be a quick work, **but the most powerful work ever done upon the earth!** I shall transform and empower My children to accomplish this work. **With Me nothing is impossible to them that believe Me and My word with everything that is within them. This truth will increase in speed and intensity as the *judgments of destruction, calamity, plague, famine, persecution and every other thing that has been prophesied, takes place.***

Fear not! The time is upon you.
Events shall move quickly
now as I have said they would.
Yahushua Ha Mashiach
Jesus The Christ

Psalm 91 (KJV)

91 He that dwelleth in the secret place of the most High shall abide under the shadow of the Almighty. 2 I will say of the Lord, He is my refuge and my fortress: my God; in him will I trust. 3 Surely he shall deliver thee from the snare of the fowler, and from the noisome pestilence. 4 He shall cover thee with his feathers, and under his wings shalt thou trust: his truth shall be thy shield and buckler. 5 Thou shalt not be afraid for the terror by night; nor for the arrow that flieth by day; 6 Nor for the pestilence that walketh in darkness; nor for the destruction that wasteth at noonday. 7 A thousand shall fall at thy side, and ten thousand at thy right hand; but it shall not come nigh thee. 8 Only with thine eyes shalt thou behold and see the reward of the wicked. 9 Because thou hast made the Lord, which is my refuge, even the most High, thy habitation; 10 There shall no evil befall thee, neither shall any plague come nigh thy dwelling. 11 For he shall give his angels charge over thee, to keep thee in all thy ways. 12 They shall bear thee up in their hands, lest thou dash thy foot against a stone. 13 Thou shalt tread upon the lion and adder: the young lion and the dragon shalt thou trample under feet. 14 Because he hath set his love upon me, therefore will I deliver him: I will set him on high, because he hath known my name. 15 He shall call upon me, and I will answer him: I will be with him in trouble; I will deliver him, and honour him. 16 With long life will I satisfy him, and shew him my salvation.

Psalm 91 Expanded Bible (EXB)

1 Those who ·go to God Most High for safety [L dwell/sit in the shelter of God Most High]
will ·be protected by [lodge in the shade/shadow of] the

Almighty.

2 I will say to the Lord, "You are my ·place of safety [refuge] and ·protection [fortress].

You are my God and I ·trust [have confidence in] you."

3 God will ·save [protect] you from ·hidden traps [L the snare of the fowler]

and from deadly ·diseases [pestilence].

4 He will cover you with his feathers,

and under his wings you ·can hide [will find refuge; Deut. 32:11; Is. 31:5; Matt. 23:37; Luke 13:34].

His ·truth [faithfulness] will be your shield and ·protection [buckler; C a small shield].

5 You will not fear any ·danger by [terror at] night

or an arrow that flies during the day.

6 ·You will not be afraid of diseases [L ...or the pestilence] that ·come [walks; stalks] in the dark

or ·sickness [L stings] that ·strikes [devastates; overpowers] at noon.

7 At your side one thousand people may ·die [L fall],

or even ten thousand ·right beside you [L at your right hand],

but ·you will not be hurt [L it will not touch you].

8 You will only ·watch [L look with your eyes]

and see the wicked ·punished [recompensed].

9 ·The Lord is your protection [L For you, Lord, are my refuge];

you have made God Most High your ·place of safety [dwelling place].

10 Nothing ·bad [evil; harmful] will ·happen to [befall] you;

no ·disaster [blow; or plague] will ·come to [approach] your ·home [L tent].

187

11 He has ·put his angels in charge of [L commanded his angels/messengers concerning] you
to ·watch over [keep; guard] ·you wherever you go [L all your ways].
12 They will ·catch you [lift you up] in their hands
so that you will not hit your foot on a rock [Matt. 4:6; Luke 4:10–11].
13 You will ·walk [tread] on lions and cobras;
you will ·step on [trample] strong lions and snakes.

14 The Lord says, "Whoever ·loves [desires] me, I will ·save [rescue].
I will ·protect [lift to safety] those who know ·me [L my name].
15 They will call to me, and I will answer them.
I will be with them in ·trouble [distress];
I will rescue them and ·honor [glorify] them.
16 I will ·give them a long, full life [L satisfy them with length of days],
and ·they will see how I can save [L show them my salvation/victory]."

Notes About the Fiery Kick-Off Event

https://holyspiritwind.net/2017/04/a-review-summary-and-order-of-the-kick-off-event-and-some-events-that-will-follow/

SUMMARY OF THE FIERY KICKOFF EVENT:

*Fiery (FIRE is involved cause He has mentioned fiery many times)

*Terrorist Attack (this means it is not from Planet X) *(He says in other writings it's New York City and preceeded by the sinking of the Abraham Lincoln vessel)*

*This is NOT from God, but it is being ALLOWED, and it has been spoken by the fallen ones AND to God's prophets. Thus, it is known by both sides.

*10 times worse than anything we've seen before. On 9/11/2001 there were over 3000 killed, the Christmas tsunami in Indonesia there were 250000 fatalities, so we can figure 30000 – 2.5Million will die.

*Economic CRASH then things seem "normal" then economic COLLAPSE

*Riots/Looting, followed by Martial law follows – but it might only follow the collapse NOT the crash (hard to tell)

*Freedoms that we enjoy now and take for granted will be gone. **The Lord has told me that freedom on the internet will be the first to go.**

*Modern conveniences and devices will be either taken away or greatly reduced shortly or immediately thereafter.

*Massive destruction like nothing we've ever seen before.

*After the event **Donald Trump will be taken away and Barack Hussein Obama will return to power** (notice I did not say he will return as POTUS) **B.H.O will then become the final anti-Christ.**

*The Third seal; the black horse, will take place which speaks of worldwide economic collapse and famine. "A quart of wheat (loaf of bread) for a denarius (days wage), and three quarts of barley for a denarius; and do not harm the oil and the wine." I believe the oil and the wine are those who are filled with the Holy Spirit. (Rev 6:5-6)

*The Fourth seal; the pale horse, "And the name of him who sat on it was Death, and Hades followed with him. And power was given to them over a fourth of the earth, to kill with sword, with hunger, with death, and by the beasts of the earth." (Rev 6 :7-8)

*It is at this time that I believe the aliens/fallen angels will come on to the scene as depicted in a vision that I had here: https://holyspiritwind.net/2016/07/kings-of-this-world-listen-to-me/

*The Fifth seal speaks of all those who have been martyred for their faith in Jesus Christ, "the word of God and for the testimony which they held. And they cried with a loud voice, saying, "How long, O Lord, holy and true, until You judge and avenge our blood on those who dwell on the earth?" Then a white robe was given to each of them; and it was said to them that they should rest a little while longer, until both the number of their fellow servants and their brethren, who would be killed as they were, was completed." (Rev 6:9-11) I believe there will be more martyrs at this time than any time before this, which is why it is placed here, some will disagree.

*The Sixth seal will occur," I looked when He opened the sixth seal, and behold, there was a great earthquake; and the sun became black as sackcloth of hair, and the moon became like blood. 13 And the stars of heaven fell to the earth, as a fig tree drops its late figs when it is shaken by a mighty wind. 14 Then the sky receded as a scroll when it is rolled up, and every mountain and island was moved out of its place. 15 And the kings of the earth, the great men, the rich men, the commanders, the mighty men, every slave and every free man, hid themselves in the caves and in the rocks of the mountains, 16 and said to the mountains and rocks, "Fall on us and hide us from the face of Him who sits on the throne and from the wrath of the Lamb! 17 For the great day of His wrath has come, and who is able to stand?" (Rev 6:12-17)

The 3 Days of darkness, the Light of the Glory of God will come down upon the people of God, the remnant, the bride, the manifest children of God, the true church, those who seek the Lord Jesus with everything that is within, then the great harvest will occur, then the rapture of the church. The rapture comes right before the wrath of God is poured out because the bride is not appointed to His wrath (1 Thess 5:9) The ones who are removed in the rapture are spoken of here, Rev 7: 13-14 "Then one of the elders answered, saying to me, "Who are these arrayed in white robes, and where did they come from?" And I said to him, "Sir, you know." So he said to me, "These are the ones who come out of the great tribulation, and washed their robes and made them white in the blood of the Lamb." After this (in my opinion) the mark of the beast will be implemented. (The order of these things will probably vary but it's my best guess!)

When the wrath of God is poured out upon the earth the devastation and destruction will be more than anyone has ever seen and the only way of repentance before the Lord Jesus will surely end in death by martyrdom or cataclysm.

Beloved, I say to you, TODAY IS THE DAY OF SALVATION! If you want to be found worthy to escape all of these things and stand before the Son of God, DO NOT WAIT!

The reason to warn about the "kickoff event" is not spread fear but just the opposite.

We all need to get ready physically, emotionally, and spiritually for this event. Spiritually ranking far above the other aspects of preparation. This can only be accomplished though total and complete surrender to the Lord Jesus Christ.

When the "kickoff event" happens there will be massive amounts of destruction, calamities, and things we have only seen in movies, but they are only the tip of the iceberg.

The whole earth will eventually BURN! Nothing you see around you will last! **The most important thing is to surrender your life to Jesus Christ (Yeshua HaMashiach) NOW!** Do not wait, seek Him with you WHOLE HEART and give Him every sin in your life. There is no sin he didn't bare on the cross and no sin He won't forgive if you repent and are sincere. Jesus said "All that the Father gives Me will come to Me, and the one who comes to Me I will by no means cast out." John 6:37

COME TO JESUS AS YOU ARE BUT DO NOT STAY THAT WAY, LET HIM TRANSFORM YOU INTO HIS LIKENESS!

Love and Peace, Jeffrey D. Byerly

WORDS & VISIONS BY MARTY BREEDEN
(Given with Permission) https://www.facebook.com/martybreeden213
April 20, 2020

With everything that is within me I believe that America's time is very limited. I do not say this lightly! As a nation, as a Superpower and as a world influence, we are on very borrowed time. First we know scripturally that Jesus said in Mark 3:24 if a Kingdom be divided against itself, that Kingdom cannot stand; Sadly America is divided spiritually, ideologically, racially, politically, and in every way! So we will not stand! In fact, I agree with David Wilkerson that we are "Mystery Babylon!" And according to Revelation 18:10: "For in one hour is thy judgment come!" The Apostle John made a point to say on 3 separate occasions concerning "Mystery Babylon" that their judgment would come in "one hour!" This nation who has been blessed with such great light of the glorious gospel has trampled upon those values unlike any nation ever has. The stench of America's sins stink in the nostrils of a

Holy God and we have offended the Holy Spirit and there is no sign of a corporate repentance, nor do I believe there will.... be although I pray it comes! This nation although being humbled is STILL arrogant and walks in darkness, and pride. Although I do believe there will be personal repentance and small pockets of revival, I pray there will be; but make no mistake America will not be great again my friends! For we have turned against that which we knew was right and true and holy and have embraced the unholy and profane and the lies I leave you with this: Do all that you can to be ready to board the "Ark Of God" which is Christ Jesus our Lord and compel your family to come aboard. I believe the clock is ticking and we have very little time left. The Bible says in Matthew 6:19-21: "Lay not up for yourselves treasures upon the Earth where moth and rust doth corrupt and and where thieves break through and steal; But lay up for yourselves treasures in heaven where neither moth nor dust doth corrupt and where thieves do not break through nor steal! For where your treasure is there will your heart be also!"

TORNADO DREAM
October 23, 2019:

First allow me to preface this dream by saying that for many years the Lord would show me a tornado in a dream to warn me of things personally, that we're going to come against me and it was always 100% accurate!

I would have a tornado dream at night, and quite often within a matter of days, sometime within a matter of hours something would surely come against me, but I had been warned by the tornado dream.

Last night for the first time in years I saw a large TORNADO!!! There were warning sirens and I could even hear the Watchmen in the background warning, yelling to the people to "RUN!!!!....RUN!!!!......RUN!!!"

Some people heeded the warnings and ran for safety and cover, yet others paid no attention but continued to walk around as if nothing was coming!! Some even walked directly into the tornado itself, despite the sirens despite the warnings, they walked directly into its path!!!

This was odd portion of the dream but I saw people's wallets and purses flying everywhere and I can see pictures of their loved ones and credit cards and money and everything being swept up in this VORTEX !!!

It was stunning to see the magnitude of this tornado and the damage caused!! Some, as they THEMSELVES were being caught up in the vortex, STILL seemed to pay no attention, that they were being utterly destroyed and continued on their daily routine ignoring that they were about to be seconds away from death.....

In my mind I remember thinking:

"Why aren't they calling out for salvation?
Why aren't they calling out to be saved?"
"WHY are they not calling out out to the Lord???"
"All is ending for them yet they will not, EVEN NOW humble themselves even in the midst of this great tragedy!!"......

I awoke....I believe a SUDDEN but power Tornado type VORTEX is about to hit this nation and this world...So many are NOT PREPARED!!!!! And it WILL catch them unaware!!!

8-20-2018 Dream
"Unexpected Storms"

Last night I had a dream that I was outside with my family. We seemed to be enjoying good family time together. Then suddenly, unexpectedly and without any warning, there was a huge BOOM of thunder...(even now I can hear it!) It shook everything around us including the ground upon which we stood. The skies immediately became a blueish black, very darkened. I recall thinking; "I always watch for these things, this is so unexpected, this came out of NOWHERE!!??" Then it began to rain, as it were, just buckets of rain. There appeared to be immediate flooding, within moments!! There were several tornados swirling all around! (These tornados have always been a warning to me of impending events!)

You could hear them but only see them shortly due to the heavy rain. The wind was blowing at an unimaginable speed!!! Then, and most significant was the LIGHTENING!!! It literally exploded with a huge boom right in front of my family, in fact we seemed to actually have been hit!! The colors were magnificent!! It produced colors...Colors that I have never even seen before!!! Again this shook the very foundations of the ground we were standing on!! Immediately though I realized that we were still alive!!!.....It was as if then I heard a voice say: "TURN AND WATCH THE TWO HOUSES BEHIND YOU!" I turned around and there was again that great crack of lightning and thunder and it hit both houses DIRECTLY!!!! It literally turned them into black ashes in a second ,....as if they have been involved in a full structure fire....totally decimated !!!!! I had the deep sense that in the midst of all these chaotic storms, that the Peace of God was in my heart and we were preserved and spared.....although the damage was incalculable all around. I awoke......

3-11-18

DREAM OF OVERWHELMING DEVASTATION X 2

It was almost as though in both the natural and in the Spirit, we were being WARNED. The people KNEW, they had been WARNED....I knew I had been WARNED. I had been WARNED by God and had warned many others as instructed by God. It was almost like we were being foretold of that which was coming as we looked at the map. There was not a single state that was not affected by these approaching storms.

From the West Coast to the East Coast to the Midlands, EVERYONE would see devastation. Even now I can see the map. I can see the swirling colors gathering. What's odd is that, normally, as the Meteorologist would show on the radar that which was coming and use different colors symbolizing severity.....they LITERALLY RAN OUT OF COLORS to be able to accurately describe that which would HIT!!!!! I can hear even now, as they foretold and trying to tell the people to **"Oh please my God prepare and know that EVEN your preparation may not save you!"**

(Now admittedly here's the part I don't understand; but will report what I saw and heard!)

They said there were six (6) storms coming. These storms had each been given names. This time they were given names of animals and birds, as to how each would affect the land and the people. We were told that the first storm would be as a bird, that it would peck away at everything, and shake things mightily, but would also be used to deliver the message as in days of old.....

(I cannot recall the 2nd storms name)

They told us that we would experience the end of all things when the WOLF came, and it was the 3rd Storm. They showed us on the map. Through tears and stuttering and hanging their heads, they told us to prepare!!!! One of the last things they said before they went off air was...."We really have nothing to compare this to, ...must get ready because you have never seen anything like this BEFORE!"

THAT NIGHT IT HIT!!!!!

Storm #1......It hit with a magnitude that no one expected! I remember that I could not gather myself enough to discern if this was natural or man-made because it literally seemed to be BOTH simultaneously!!!! The winds, the rain, the wreckage, everything........I recall watching the large trees bending under the weight of the wind and seeing the waters rising on the coast and seeing the heartland POUNDED by a mighty force. The next morning ....just as it was named it had pecked and shaken everything and word had indeed traveled across country at the devastation that had occurred. Now......it was time to move on to the next storm warning. (This is where it gets tough!)

Again, we looked at the map and literally we ALL GASPED as we saw the size and scope of what was coming KNOWING the magnitude of the first. This time, all they would say was,.... "We really don't know what to say or how to warn, just prepare as best you can!" The next day....IT HIT!!!! During the daylight hours it came. It was really odd for you could see the storm clouds gathering and you could literally hear it coming. I remember seeing the looks of fear and dread on people's faces. Some people prayed, others checked their supplies. For one of the first times ever though, it seemed as though now everyone was taking the warnings to heart and there was little to no mockery.....the first storm had taken care of all that. The power by which this storm hit is truly unexplainable! Every foundation was shaken, every room of every house had been MOVED! I saw Naval Destroyers literally CAPSIZED on dry ground far from the coast from where they had come!!!I saw death and destruction in unprecedented ways. There was not a single family, business or church that had not been affected and devastated. I recall back now that while it was happening, that I expected to be swept away any second.....i expected to be standing before my Lord any moment. The cries of pain and heartache was nothing I want to hear again. Again, the wind, the rain, the SHAKING, the sounds of explosions and waters rising and ground splitting and seeing ocean waters flowing through rivers......

I recall after storm #2 had hit thinking, now I know why Jesus said those days must be cut short for if they were not, no flesh would be saved!! I remember thinking; "My God, this is only storm 2 of 6.....all of humanity and all the earth will be WIPED OUT and the earth disintegrate beneath our feet!!!!" Even those most prepared among us, MANY of them perished for there appeared in most cases to be no escape. There were Godly among us who had been taken......along with many of those who were not believers. I noticed though, even as I surveyed the landscape the following day... I could not believe the devastation and damage. EVERYTHING had indeed been shaken JUST AS foretold by Christ!! The one thing I saw that surprised me was that now, it seemed there was very few if any who did not believe. Everyone was broken in a way unforeseen. A level of brokenness I had never witnessed....EVER! Amidst the tragedy and devastation and carnage there arose a brokenness among the people.....for they knew that it was only a matter of time. It was then that we gathered to hear the next forecast....we were all so tired and so weary, but there was a deep work going in in the heart of man...God was at Work! This would be the "WOLF" coming this time.

As the forecaster took the stage he was VISIBLY SHAKEN! .....but not in despondency this time....something was different. He stood before the camera, gathered himself as best he could and I heard Him say these words....."The people are REPENTING!"....."THE PEOPLE ARE REPENTING!" He then said....."And it's because of this repentance that...Well, look at these storms NOW!!.....Yes, they are still coming but they have been dramatically weakened and will not cause the devastation we had originally anticipated!!" This reporter wept on national television....I recall myself and all those around me weeping and praising God!!! Me being me....my mind went immediately to "Ok, it's time NOW to gather the harvest!!!!.......The fields are white unto harvest...let us go forth now and bring them IN!! ...

I AWOKE.....

September 4, 2019
Beast Meeting

Last night I had a dream where I saw many of the worlds professing "Elites" meeting. I saw governmental leaders, religious leaders, and many advisers. In a clear mockery of supposed purity, they all dressed in white, but in this dream the Lord allowed me to see that in fact, these people had very dark hearts. I recognized many of them, some I had never seen before. There was truly a sense of unholy unity among them. I was only allowed to hear certain portions of their discussion. I know that they were talking about creating very hard times specifically for Israel and the Jewish people. As they spoke about this subject in particular, there was a demonic and visceral hatred in their speech and on their faces. The conversation then turned to world chaos and the steps that would be systematically taken to create havoc and to increase pressure on Christians worldwide.

Again, it seemed as though their faces contorted with hatred speaking of Christian's. There were to be coming events, even orchestrated events that would cause world opinion to begin to turn against that which they were against. There was a time during the dream that I could feel fear and even anger begin to grab my heart....It was at that moment though, that it seemed I could hear the soft voice of Jesus, the "Shepherd and Bishop of our souls" speak to my heart: "Yes, Yes, I see it all, do not fear! Let not your heart be troubled, trust Me in the coming days, in the midst of these events, you will still have my peace and my comfort! Remind my children that I am making intercession for them!" I awoke.....

Marty's Testimony on
https://www.victoryembracedministries.org/blog/tag/marty-breeden

At one time, as a young man of 17, I had given my heart to the Lord with great passion. As in many cases though—I got busy with life. In 2015, at 51 years of age, those years of experiencing the zeal of the Lord seemed far away. I had no idea how the Lord was about to sternly, yet lovingly, bring me back to Himself. On July 17, 2015, as a result of my going into acute respiratory failure, I went "Code Blue". I would go "Code Blue" yet again within 48 hours. When I "coded" the first time, I immediately left my body, and I found myself standing in what I sensed was the presence of the Lord. Thinking back now, there were a million things He could have said to me, and what He did say, I was certainly not expecting. With an imminence and urgency beyond description, He said, "MY CHURCH DOES NOT REALLY BELIEVE THAT I'M COMING BACK SOON!" He repeated this two more times, as I stood there in stunned silence. Each time, it was with more volume and more passion. I finally said, waving my hands like a school child to get His attention, "Lord, yes we do believe you're coming back soon.

We sing about it, pray about it, study about it; yes, Lord, we do believe that you're coming back soon!" He then said, "MY Church does not really believe I'm coming back soon, for if they did, they would not be living as they are!" Then, I listened as the timbre of His voice changed. He said, "I AM coming back soon, and my Church is not ready...Now, go back and tell the things that you have heard, and know that your message will not be received!" I was in the CCU for three weeks, the majority of that on a respirator with a tracheotomy. I survived and would go to the University of Virginia Transitional Care Facility to learn how to walk, talk, and swallow again. It was there, that I had a second encounter with the Lord on August 14, 2015. In a night vision, He spoke to me these words: "My church should be living as though this is the TWO-MINUTE WARNING!" Being a huge football fan, I knew exactly what He was saying:

That we should be working with absolute purpose and passion, because in that Two-Minute Warning, those last 120 seconds can determine victory or defeat. It's an all-out rush to do all you can to win the game, to put up a strong offense, and—if you're winning—to keep the opposition from gaining ground or scoring points. As the Apostle Paul said, "I was not disobedient to the heavenly vision." Those encounters changed my life, and as I lovingly warn the Church, I see this message changing the hearts of others as well. I now go to the highways and byways and compel men to come in. I often pray that in the time I have remaining that I will live a life that will make sense in the light of eternity. With all that is within me, I know He is coming, and I believe His blessed return to be nearer than most would believe. Get your houses in order; ask the Holy Spirit for guidance and leading as to what you are supposed to be doing in this late; late hour. Surely, our "redemption draweth nigh" (Luke 21:28 KJV).

8

Preparations for

Judgment

Now that we recognize the judgment is coming and what we did to bring judgment, the next thing we must consider is "How do we prepare for it? What do I need to do to leave this apostasy, etc."? The Bible tells us to touch not the unclean thing. We must not be attached to the world when it hits.

Believe me Bride, when we are attached to something or someone that is false, when the judgment hits them, it will affect everything it's attached to. Remember what I shared about Lot and Abraham's judgment in Sodom and Gomorrah? Everything that sin touched in that city got destroyed.

GET OUT OF THE POLLUTED WATERS!

GET IN THE CLEAR RIVERS FROM THE THRONE OF GOD!

MASS EXODUS OF THE BRIDE

First thing we must do is examine our hearts. We need to examine our lives. Now that we know what the apostasy is, we must ask the Holy Spirit how to separate from it and detach. We must set in our hearts that nothing or no one is going to come in between me and God. Remember that this is in opposite of what they're teaching out there right now with that ecumenical movement, universalism and the "common good", "community", etc. **CHOOSE THIS DAY WHO YOU WILL SERVE.** We need to detach ourselves from the apostasy!

Remember Bride that God is warning us so that we can get our houses in order while we have time.

HOW TO PREPARE FOR THE JUDGMENT

1. **Prepare Your Families**
    a. Talk to them about the apostasy and the judgment coming. Warn them to get out while they can!
    b. Educate them on the end of times and tell them that time is approaching.
    c. Tell them that Jesus loves them and created them to live FOR SUCH A TIME AS THIS. It is nothing to fear.
    d. Read the Bible with them. Cause them to love the word. <u>We may not have it much longer.</u>
    e. Do disaster preparedness drills with them. Setup an action plan.
        i. Who to call if phones are working
        ii. What to do if phones and grid goes down
        iii. Where to get water and how to survive
        iv. Who to trust, etc.

      v. Write it out on a piece of paper what to do and instructions so that if computers go out you have a piece of paper of instructions

      vi. Get maps! Get paper maps of cities

      vii. Find out where some Cities of Refuge are

  f. Is your family ready to protect themselves?

      i. Do you have guns? How will you protect your homes?

      ii. Do you have a bunker for storms?

2. Prepare Your Home

  a. First thing is praying a wall of fire around your dwelling

      i. Pray the fire ALL THE WAY TO THE CORE OF THE EARTH AND TO THE HEAVENS

      ii. This will cover and help through natural disasters. At the end of this book I have a prayer for that

  b. Stock up on food and water.

      i. Make sure you find a good hiding place because people will try to come in and steal it.

      ii. Maybe you can find a room and hide it in the walls, etc.

      iii. Remember that if the grid goes down (all electronics and power) that you will not be able to flush your toilets, etc. So, you need to have a backup of toilet services (maybe a bucket and somewhere to dump.

  c. Make sure your family knows which house you will all go to when this happens.

  d. Make sure you are all filled with the Holy Ghost. I

truly believe this is how we are going to communicate one day.

  i. I consider the Book of Acts. They didn't have electronics back then and God would give them dreams, etc., and lead them.

 e. Stock up on batteries, candles, etc.

3. Prepare Your Heart!

 a. Do not be afraid or allow fear in. God knew he created you for this. He knew the timing of all this.

 b. There is not one person in the Bible that God called that he did not help them and lead them through whatever he told them to do. So, don't be afraid.

 c. Encourage your family and friends to not be afraid.

 d. Read the Bible and get to know God more intimately so that when all this happens it won't throw you off. You will already have a relationship with him.

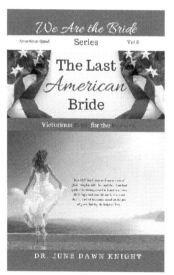

Make sure you know who you can trust Bride. This is key.

My next book, *The Last American Bride* will address where do we go from here.

Works Cited

AD Blog. (2017, October 31). *Kenneth Copeland Calls for End of the Protestant Reformation*. Retrieved from Amazing Discoveries: https://amazingdiscoveries.org/blog/kenneth-copeland-calls-end-protestant-reformation/

ADF. (2018, May 16). *Court orders end to abortion-pill mandate for Oklahoma Christian universities*. Retrieved from Alliance Defending Freedom - ADF Legal: https://www.adflegal.org/detailspages/press-release-details/court-orders-end-to-abortion-pill-mandate-for-oklahoma-christian-universities

AFA. (2017, March 27). *Are Sanctuary Cities Like Biblical Cities of Refuge?* Retrieved from American Family Association: https://www.afa.net/the-stand/culture/2017/03/are-sanctuary-cities-like-biblical-cities-of-refuge/

AHA. (2016, September 16). *Implantable Medical Devices*. Retrieved from Heart.org: http://www.heart.org/HEARTORG/Conditions/HeartAttack/TreatmentofaHeartAttack/Implantable-Medical-Devices_UCM_303940_Article.jsp#.WuNN18gvzIU

Aliff, A. (2018, April 18). *Symptoms of Kundalini Awakening*. Retrieved from The Awakened State: http://theawakenedstate.tumblr.com/post/141572026380/symptoms-of-kundalini-awakening-1-strongly

Aliff, A. (2018, April 18). *Symptoms of Awakening*. Retrieved from The Awakened State: https://theawakenedstate.net/kundalini-awakening/symptoms-of-awakening/

Amazon. (2018, April 26). *Amazon PrimeAir*. Retrieved from
    Amazon.com: https://www.amazon.com/Amazon-Prime-
    Air/b?ie=UTF8&node=8037720011

Apologetics Index. (2018, March 24). *Manifested Sons of God*. Retrieved
    from Apologetics Index:
    http://www.apologeticsindex.org/m22.html

Arnott, N. (2013, February 25). *Privacy and security in the age of iPhone
    mics and cameras*. Retrieved from iMore:
    https://www.imore.com/privacy-and-security-age-mobile-mics-
    and-cameras

Bethel Church. (2018, January 08). *Christalignment*. Retrieved from
    Bethel Church: http://www.bethel.com/about/christalignment/

Bethel Ministries. (2018, March 27). *Bethel School of Technology*.
    Retrieved from Bethel Tech: https://betheltech.net/

BGEA STAFF. (2013, September 10). *Answers - Why Did Adam & Eve Eat
    the Apple?* Retrieved from Billy Graham:
    https://billygraham.org/answer/why-did-adam-and-eve-eat-
    that-apple-didnt-they-know-it-was-wrong-and-was-going-to-
    bring-them-all-sorts-of-trouble/

Bickle, M. (2001, July 19). *Contemplative Prayer*. Retrieved from
    mikebickle.org:
    https://drive.google.com/drive/u/0/folders/1C4zDUpQ-
    jR5nO6kuGUkjhIbzx4kk1Nj1

Bill Johnson. (2000, July 21). *Bill Johnson Quotes*. Retrieved from Bethel
    Music: https://bethelmusic.com/blog/bill-johnson-quotes/

Boston Dynamics. (2018). *About*. Retrieved from BostonDynamics.com:
    https://www.bostondynamics.com/about

Bounds, E. (1984). *Gu ide to Spiritual Warfare*. New Kinsington, PA: whitaker House.

Britannica. (2018, April 08). *Mystcism*. Retrieved from Britannica Encyclopedia: https://www.britannica.com/topic/mysticism

Brynjolfsson, E., & McAfee, A. (2017, July). *The Business of Artificial Intelligence - What it can - and cannot - do for your organization*. Retrieved from Harvard Business Review: https://hbr.org/cover-story/2017/07/the-business-of-artificial-intelligence

Cambridge. (2018, May 16). *Definitions*. Retrieved from Cambridge Dictionary: https://dictionary.cambridge.org/us/dictionary/english/recant

CBN. (2018, April 06). *Baptism in the Holy Spirit*. Retrieved from CBN: http://www1.cbn.com/spirituallife/what-is-baptism-in-the-holy-spirit

Channel, S. (2017, June 12). *Here's How Holograms On Stage Can Look So Real*. Retrieved from YouTube.com: https://www.youtube.com/watch?v=luNj_rqx04o

Christalignment. (2018, March 27). *Christalignment*. Retrieved from Christalignment: http://www.christalignment.org/

Christians Together. (2011, February 17). *Kingdom Now teaching: beware*. Retrieved from Christians Together in the Highlands and Islands: https://www.christianstogether.net/Articles/244590/Christians _Together_in/Survival_Kit/Kingdom_Now_teaching.aspx

Christmas, K. (2018, January 4). *Prophetic Word for 2018*. Retrieved from YouTube: "For Christians who no longer value My presence anymore and are lukewarm and My

Coppenger, M. (2008, May 29). *Oprah & a Jealous God*. Retrieved from
Baptist Press: http://www.bpnews.net/28150/oprah-and-a-
jealous-god

Cortes, A. (2017, September 12). *After-school Satan club tests the limits
of church and state*. Retrieved from KALW Local Public Ratio:
http://kalw.org/post/after-school-satan-club-tests-limits-
church-and-state#stream/0

Dallas Morning News Editorial. (2017, June 1). *Editorials - T.D. Jakes'
Shark Tank - style competition will teach skills Dallas kids need.*
Retrieved from Dallas News:
https://www.dallasnews.com/opinion/editorials/2017/06/01/e
ncouragement-home-grown-entrepreneurs

DeBruyn, L. (2014, August 29). *The Physics of Heaven: A Serial Book
Review & Theological Interaction: Pt 1*. Retrieved from
Herescope: http://herescope.blogspot.com/2014/08/the-
physics-of-heaven.html?m=1

Deitsch, R. (2018, January 03). *NFL Ratings Decline ESPN, Fox, NBC
Network TV*. Retrieved from Sports Illustrated:
https://www.si.com/tech-media/2018/01/03/nfl-ratings-
decline-espn-fox-nbc-network-tv

Del Ray, J. (2018, February 06). *Alphabet's drone delivery division has
added an Amazon veteran to its leadership team*. Retrieved
from Recode.net:
https://www.recode.net/2018/2/6/16965834/google-drone-
project-wing-faisal-masud-amazon-alphabet

Democracy NOW. (2017, January 04). *Privacy Advocates Warn of
Potential Surveillance Through Listening Devices Like Amazon
Echo*. Retrieved from YouTube.com:
https://www.youtube.com/watch?v=zX1owl7cmDA

Dewey, K. (2016, November 3). *Desert Prophet - Ken Dewey*. Retrieved from Facebook: https://www.facebook.com/1632834926950237/photos/a.1632 870040280059.1073741828.1632834926950237/18813717987 63214/?type=3&theater

Dewey, K. (2018, May 20). *End Time Warnings*. Retrieved from Facebook: https://www.facebook.com/ken.dewey2/posts/1021121714755 8372

Diamond. (2018, April 26). *Diamond and Silk Congressional Testimony*. Retrieved from Facebook.com: https://www.facebook.com/DiamondandSilk/videos/10625653 23892580/

EAUK. (2018). *Search Results for Ecumenical*. Retrieved from EAUK.org: http://www.eauk.org/search-results-filter.cfm?incl_subsites=0&showSummaryCheckBox=0&UserSel ectedSubSites=&startpage=1&curpage=1&srchString=ecumenic al

Elgan, M. (2018, January 20). *The future of 3D holograms comes into focus*. Retrieved from ComputerWorld.com: https://www.computerworld.com/article/3249605/virtual-reality/the-future-of-3d-holograms-comes-into-focus.html

Erdmann, M. (2013, December 21). *What Is Dominionism?* Retrieved from Deception in the Church: http://www.deceptioninthechurch.com/ditc47-2.html

Fisher, C. (2015, January 07). *Bethel Music; a Work of Darkness*. Retrieved from Truth Keepers: http://www.truthkeepers.com/?p=754

Fowler, B. (2018, January 29). *Mobile Technology: What You Need to Know About 5G*. Retrieved from Consumer Reports: https://www.consumerreports.org/mobile-technology/what-you-need-to-know-about-5g/

Foxe, J. (2018, March 22). *Fox's Book of Martyrs.* Retrieved from The Project Gutenberg: http://ihtys.narod.ru/foxes_book_of_martyrs.pdf

FX. (2018, May 20). *Legion - About the Show*. Retrieved from FX Now: http://www.fxnetworks.com/shows/legion

Genome.gov. (2017, March 21). *Cloning Fact Sheet*. Retrieved from genome.gov: https://www.genome.gov/25020028/cloning-fact-sheet/

GodTV. (2018). *About*. Retrieved from GodTV: https://www.god.tv/about/

GodTV. (2018). *About Alpha*. Retrieved from GodTV: https://www.god.tv/vod/alpha/

Gong, G. (2013, February 20). *Securing RFID Systems Using Lightweight Stream Cipher*. Retrieved from Microsoft.com: https://www.microsoft.com/en-us/research/video/securing-rfid-systems-using-lightweight-stream-cipher/

Graham, B. (1974). *Billy Graham Speech at 1st Confress*. Retrieved from Lausanne: https://www.lausanne.org/content/why-lausanne-print

Hamill, J. (2018, April 10). *METRO Facebook can predict people's behaviour by spying through their smartphone, patent reveals.* Retrieved from Metro News.uk: http://metro.co.uk/2018/04/10/facebook-can-predict-peoples-behaviour-spying-smartphone-patent-reveals-7452861/?ito=cbshare

Harris, E. A. (2017, October 26). *Tattoos, Bieber, Black Lives Matter and Jesus*. Retrieved from New York Times: https://www.nytimes.com/2017/10/26/books/hillsong-church-carl-lentz-book-justin-bieber.html

Herescope. (2007, July 09). *As in Heaven So on Earth*. Retrieved from Herescope: http://herescope.blogspot.com/2007/07/as-in-heaven-so-on-earth.html

Herrin, J. (2014, June 03). *Deception - Part 4*. Retrieved from Parables; Bringing Hidden Truths to Light: http://parablesblog.blogspot.com/2014/06/deception-part-4.html

Hiltzik, M. (2016, August 19). *The Supreme Court's awful Hobby Lobby decision just spawned a very ugly stepchild*. Retrieved from LA Times: http://www.latimes.com/business/hiltzik/la-fi-hiltzik-hobby-child-20160819-snap-story.html

Huawei. (2015). *5G Vision: 100 Billion connections, 1 ms Latency, and 10 Gbps Throughput*. Retrieved from Huawei.com: http://www.huawei.com/minisite/5g/en/defining-5g.html

Huawei. (2018). *About - Invitation*. Retrieved from Huawei.com: http://www.huawei.com/minisite/has2018/en/about.html

ICAL. (2018, April 08). *Statement of Faith*. Retrieved from ICAL Leaders: https://www.icaleaders.com/about-ical/statement-of-faith

ImageNet. (2016). *About ImageNet*. Retrieved from ImageNet: http://image-net.org/about-overview

Jefferies, M. (2017, July 17). *Hillsong, Bethel Music and The Great Seduction*. Retrieved from Emergent Watch: https://emergentwatch.com/2017/07/17/hillsong-bethel-music-and-the-great-seduction/

Johnson, B. (2003, January 01). *When Heaven Invades Earth*. Retrieved from Google Books: https://play.google.com/store/books/details/Bill_Johnson_When_Heaven_Invades_Earth?id=msDOo0EM6ucC

Johnson, B. (2014, April 11). *Don't Worship the Bible - Bill Johnson*. Retrieved from YouTube: https://www.youtube.com/watch?time_continue=26&v=J5Bh5NMyhyA

Johnson, B. (2017, May 13). *A Mess- Heidi Baker - Bill Johnson - Rolland Baker - Bethel Redding*. Retrieved from YouTube: https://www.youtube.com/watch?v=vbEpJU1UMR0

Joyner, R. (2006, April 01). *"Taking the Land--The Coming Kingdom"*. Retrieved from Elijah List: http://www.elijahlist.com/words/display_word.html?ID=3948

Keckler, C. (1999). *From Convent to Pentecost*. Retrieved from Christian Hospitality: http://www.christianhospitality.org/resources/charlotte-convent-to-pentecost.pdf

Knight, D. J. (2020, April 19). What Is The Beast? Merging Of Government, Economy & Religion – AI, IoT, Etc. Retrieved from WATB.tv: https://watb.tv/what-is-the-beast-merging-of-government-economy-religion-ai-iot-etc/?fbclid=IwAR38hTMlmeM1zMMS_nV-CJ7nR0imPhNoHGdgDX_LXcZywLXsc2gRlNcwdYl

KOHLER, P. (2016, September 19). *What Is Kingdom Now Theology?* Retrieved from Salvation and Survival: https://www.salvationandsurvival.com/2016/09/what-is-kingdom-now-theology.html

Kozar, S. (2016, February 1). *The Charismatic Day of Infamy: June 23rd 2008*. Retrieved from Pirate Christian: http://www.piratechristian.com/messedupchurch/2016/2/the- charismatic-day-of-infamy-june-28th-2008

Lang, N. (2017, March 21). *Disney's Long, Complicated History with Queer Characters*. Retrieved from Harpers Bazaar: https://www.harpersbazaar.com/culture/film-tv/news/a21506/disney-gay-lgbt-characters-history/

Lausanne.org. (2018, April 08). *Our Legacy*. Retrieved from Lausanne Movement: https://www.lausanne.org/our-legacy

Lloyd, A. B. (2018, March 15). *Congressman: Child Sex Dolls Are Coming—And We're Not Ready*. Retrieved from WeeklyStandard.com: https://www.weeklystandard.com/alice-b-lloyd/congressman-child-sex-dolls-are-coming-mdash-and-were-not-ready

Lutz, A. (2012, June 14). *These 6 Corporations Control 90% Of The Media In America*. Retrieved from Business Insider: http://www.businessinsider.com/these-6-corporations-control-90-of-the-media-in-america-2012-6

Marans, D. (2016, August 18). *Target To Install Gender-Neutral Bathrooms In All Of Its Stores*. Retrieved from Huffinton Post Magazine: https://www.huffingtonpost.com/entry/target-single-stall-bathrooms_us_57b4b6bfe4b0fd5a2f40dee8

Maryam Rajavi. (2018). *AGAINST ISLAMIC EXTREMISM RULING IN IRAN*. Retrieved from Mayam Rajavi: https://www.maryam-rajavi.com/en/viewpoints/iran-islamic-fundamentalism

Maryam Rajavi. (2018). *IRAN REGIME CHANGE - THE THIRD OPTION*. Retrieved from Maryam Rajavi: https://www.maryam-rajavi.com/en/viewpoints/iran-regime-change

Maryam Rajavi. (2018). *THE FACE OF THE FUTURE DEMOCRATIC IRAN*. Retrieved from Maryam Rajavi: https://www.maryam-rajavi.com/en/viewpoints/future-iran

Mattera, J. (2017, January 17). *Last Days Views That Lead To Semi-Gnosticism*. Retrieved from Joseph Mattera: http://josephmattera.org/last-days-views-that-lead-to-semi-gnosticism/

McCumber, M. (2012, August 26). *Taking Dominion- Do We Really Want God's Kingdom Now?* Retrieved from Deception Bytes: http://deceptionbytes.com/taking-dominion-do-we-really-want-gods-kingdom-now/

McLaughlin, E. C. (2017, April 26). *Suspect OKs Amazon to hand over Echo recordings in murder case*. Retrieved from CNN.com: https://www.cnn.com/2017/03/07/tech/amazon-echo-alexa-bentonville-arkansas-murder-case/index.html

MegaFest. (2018). *Destiny World*. Retrieved from MegaFest: http://www.mega-fest.org/destinyworld/

Moody, G. (2015,). *DEMONIC CHILD ENTERTAINMENT*. Retrieved from Demon Buster: http://www.demonbuster.com/demonicc.html

Muir, D. (2018, April 25). *04/25/18: 'Golden State Killer' Suspect Arrested*. Retrieved from ABC.go.com: http://abc.go.com/shows/world-news-tonight/episode-guide/2018-04/25-042518-golden-state-killer-suspect-arrested

NAIOTH COLLEGE. (2017, August 22). *Tribe Byron Bay*. Retrieved from Facebook: https://www.facebook.com/tribebyronbay/photos/a.19695598 0468162.1073741827.196944577135969/802205536609867/?t ype=3&theater

NAOITH College. (2017, August 21). *NAOITH College*. Retrieved from Facebook.com: https://www.facebook.com/tribebyronbay/photos/a.196955980468162.1073 741827.196944577135969/802205536609867/?type=3&theater

Neergaard, L. (2018, January 24). *Tiny Implant Opens Way to Deliver Drugs Deep Into the Brain.* Retrieved from Associated Press: https://www.apnews.com/9760860d3d9a42598e09c4c3e67831 22/Tiny-implant-opens-way-to-deliver-drugs-deep-into-the-brain

NEWS DIVISION. (2018, March 27). *Charismatics Now Using "Christian" Tarot Cards.* Retrieved from Pulpit and Pen: http://pulpitandpen.org/2017/12/11/charismatics-now-using-christian-tarot-cards/

NIBIB. (2018, March 5). *News & Events.* Retrieved from National Institute of Biomedical Imaging and Bioengineering: https://www.nibib.nih.gov/news-events/newsroom/tiny-implant-opens-way-deliver-drugs-deep-brain

nl, B. f. (2018, March 27). *Monstrance.* Retrieved from Wiki Media: https://commons.wikimedia.org/wiki/File:Monstrans.jpg

Oakland, R. (2004). *Another Jesus? The eucharistic Christ and the New Evangelization.* Silverton, OR: Lighthouse Trails Publishing.

Oakland, R. (2007). *Faith Undone.* Eureka, Montana: Lighthouse Trails Publishing.

Odle, D. (1998). *Grace Abuse; One of the Greatest Hindrances to Genuine Revival.* Write Hand Publishing.

Odle, D. (2012). *The Polluted Church; From Rome to Kansas City.* Opelika, AL: BookBaby.

Oliver, M. (1996, July 16). *Eddy Manson; Noted Harmonica Player.* Retrieved from LA T imes: http://articles.latimes.com/1996-07-16/news/mn-24749_1_harmonica-player

O'NEIL, M. (2018, April 09). *Sex robots could 'change humanity forever': Expert warns the rise of realistic dolls may 'take meaning out of our lives' by making sex 'too easy'*. Retrieved from DailyMail.co.uk: http://www.dailymail.co.uk/sciencetech/article-5595863/Researcher-warns-sex-robots-change-humanity-forever.html

Oppenheimer, M. (2011, May 27). *The Church of Oprah Winfrey and a Theology of Suffering*. Retrieved from The New York Times: https://www.nytimes.com/2011/05/28/us/28beliefs.html

Pearson, C. (2018). *Carlton Pearson*. Retrieved from BishopPearson.com: http://www.bishoppearson.com/

Quayle, S. (2018, April 05). *Steve Quayle Interview April 05 2018| Your King Is Coming*. Retrieved from YouTube: https://www.youtube.com/watch?v=feFnoTYuV2I

Quayle, S. (2018, April 26). *TERMINATED! The End of Man Is Here- Steve Quayle*. Retrieved from YouTube.com: https://youtu.be/wQpDtTkLc04

Quora. (2018, February 02). *The Difference Between Virtual Reality, Augmented Reality And Mixed Reality*. Retrieved from Forbes.com: https://www.forbes.com/sites/quora/2018/02/02/the-difference-between-virtual-reality-augmented-reality-and-mixed-reality/#62d7ce892d07

Reagan, D. D. (2018, April 28). *The One World Religion*. Retrieved from ChristinProphecy.com: http://christinprophecy.org/articles/the-one-world-religion/

Régimbal, F. J.-P. (2015, October 23). *Examples of Subliminal Messages in Rock Music*. Retrieved from Tradition in Action:
http://www.traditioninaction.org/Cultural/D054_Rock_4.htm

Ride Conference. (2018). *Ride Conference - Innovative Change Agents*. Retrieved from Ride Conference: https://ride.rollingout.com/

Robinson, J. (2014, October 9). *Wife of GOD TV founder who quit over 'moral failure' says he left her for South African farmer's divorcee daughter - and 'the devil got in very, very easily'* .

Retrieved from Daily Mail:
http://www.dailymail.co.uk/news/article-2786459/Wife-GOD-TV-founder-quit-moral-failure-says-left-South-African-farmer-s-divorcee-daughter-devil-got-easily.html#ixzz5GwEZKtnk

RobotLAB. (2018, April 28). *NAO V5 Standard Edition - Robots for Developers*. Retrieved from RobotLab.com:
https://www.robotlab.com/store/nao-standard-edition

Silva, K. (2014, May 19). *A SECOND PENTECOST: IS THERE THE HOPE OF AN END-TIME REPEAT OF PENTECOST?!* Retrieved from
Apprising Ministries: http://apprising.org/2014/05/19/a-second-pentecost-is-there-the-hope-of-an-end-time-repeat-of-pentecost/

Stand Up for the Truth. (2016, June 01). *BLURRING LINES BETWEEN THE CHURCH AND THE WORLD*. Retrieved from Stand Up for the Truth: https://standupforthetruth.com/2016/06/blurring-lines-church-world/

Strom, A. (2015, September 24). *BILL JOHNSON, BETHEL & the NEW AGE*. Retrieved from John the Baptist TV:
http://www.johnthebaptisttv.com/

Summers, T. (2018, April 19). *Hellsong Satanic Baptism in Their Song "Peace"*. Retrieved from YouTube: https://www.youtube.com/watch?v=27cNi8EskaE

Suri, Y. (2014, September 24). *Gold Dust and Gems Falling From Heaven - Spiritual Adultery*. Retrieved from YouTube: https://www.youtube.com/watch?v=vb15EhgbvHA

T.D. Jakes. (2018). *Bishop T.D. Jakes*. Retrieved from T.D. Jakes: http://www.tdjakes.org/

Target. (2016, April 19). *Continuing to Stand for Inclusivity*. Retrieved from Target: https://corporate.target.com/article/2016/04/target-stands-inclusivity

TBN. (2018, May 20). *ABOUT THE PROGRAM - There is More to the Secret*. Retrieved from TBN - Trinity Broadcasting Network: https://tbn.org/programs/there-more-secret/about

TechJect. (2016, November 02). *8 ADVANCED ROBOTS ANIMAL YOU NEED TO SEE*. Retrieved from YouTube.com: https://www.youtube.com/watch?v=voNBzuI7IJ4

Techject. (2018). *Our History*. Retrieved from Techject.com: http://techject.com/us/

Trafton, A. (2015, November 18). *A New Way to Monitor Vital Signs; Ingestible sensor measures heart and breathing rates from within the digestive tract*. Retrieved from MIT.edu: http://news.mit.edu/2015/ingestible-sensor-measures-heart-breathing-rates-1118

TruNews. (2017, December 20). *Bethel Pastor Defends Use of Destiny Cards*. Retrieved from TruNews: https://www.trunews.com/article/update-bethel-pastor-defends-use-of-destiny-cards

TruNews. (2017, December 15). *California Megachurch Dabbling in Occult*. Retrieved from TruNews: https://www.trunews.com/article/california-megachurch-dabbling-in-occult

Truth in Reality. (2012, September 21). *What is Kingdom Theology and the Kingdom Now Teaching?* Retrieved from Truth in Reality: https://truthinreality.com/2012/09/21/what-is-kingdom-theology-and-the-kingdom-now-teaching/

Truthunedited. (2018, Feb 23). *BLACK PANTHER EXPOSED: Witchcraft Served to the Black Community*. Retrieved from YouTube: https://www.youtube.com/watch?v=z6trkRnenEQ

Vigilent Christian. (2016, May 24). *Hillsong London Easter Voodoo Dance Ritual Special 2016 EXPOSED!* Retrieved from YouTube:

https://www.youtube.com/watch?v=WMy1hpJ2hcg

Wax, T. (2013, May 08). *John Stott Confronted Billy Graham*. Retrieved from The Gospel Coalition: https://www.thegospelcoalition.org/blogs/trevin-wax/when-john-stott-confronted-billy-graham/

Wheeler, T. (2016, June 20). *FCC Chair Tom Wheeler speaks at The National Press Club - June 20, 2016*. Retrieved from YouTube.com: https://www.youtube.com/watch?v=tNH35Kcao60

Wikipedia. (2018, March 28). *Dominionism*. Retrieved from Wikipedia: https://en.wikipedia.org/wiki/Dominion_theology

Wikipedia. (2018, May 20). *Mr. Pickles*. Retrieved from Wikipedia: https://en.wikipedia.org/wiki/Mr._Pickles

World Council of Churches. (2018, March 27). *World Council of Churches; A worldwide fellowship of churches seeking unity, a common witness and Christian service*. Retrieved from Oikoumene: https://www.oikoumene.org/en/

World Council of Churches WCC. (2018, March 27). *GETI 2018*. Retrieved from Oikoumene: https://www.oikoumene.org/en/mission2018/geti-2018

Wyatt, R. (2007, March 07). *A NOW WORD--IT'S TIME FOR THE PROPHETIC TO BE EARTHED AND THE KINGDOM OF GOD ESTABLISHED* . Retrieved from Identity Network: http://www.identitynetwork.net/apps/articles/default.asp?articleid=31188&columnid=2093

YouTube. (2018, April 03). *Sadhu Sundar Selvaraj April 03 2018 — GOD'S JUDGEMENT ON YOUR NATION FOR SINS — Sadhu Sundar 2018*. Retrieved from YouTube: https://www.youtube.com/watch?v=aPpPs0e9j_c

ABOUT THE AUTHOR

We Are the Bride Ministries Founder

Dr. June Dawn Knight is an author, revivalist, media specialist, mother and grandmother. Her heart is to serve her community. She has been in public service for the last 15 years. She spearheaded four organizations. The Middle Tennessee Jr. League Cheerleader's Association in which she unified four different counties and ten cities for cheerleading. MTJLCA still exists today. She also served as the president of the Steelworker's Union for the CMCSS Bus Drivers in 2004/2005. Then, she went to World Harvest Bible College in Columbus, Ohio. Following Bible College, she attended APSU from 2008 – 2012. During her time at APSU, she spearheaded three organizations on campus. Dr. June Dawn served student life and served on the Provost Committee for the students. Please see the following newspaper articles and videos:

http://www.apsu.edu/news/new-organization-apsu-gives-voice-nontraditional-students

http://www.apsu.edu/news/4-apsu-students-establish-new-honor-society-nontraditional-students

http://www.apsu.edu/news/27-apsu-students-named-prestigious-whos-who-among-college-students

http://www.apsu.edu/news/apsu-annual-awards-program-honors-student-leaders-faculty-staff-organizations

http://www.discoverclarksville.com/articles/tag/june-dawn-knight/

http://www.youtube.com/watch?v=ZyvnE4epKDE

(Video of Non-Traditional Accomplishments at APSU)

http://www.youtube.com/watch?v=tV9HKJ3PFnI

(NTSS Commercial)

http://www.youtube.com/watch?v=9bjBM28lpVk

(Austin's Angels TV Show)

http://www.youtube.com/watch?v=u_b0nbDZ9uI

(My Retirement from MTJLCA)

Dr. June Dawn graduated APSU in December 2012 with her master's Degree in Corporate Communication. She studied in London during Grad School under the top three global Public Relations/Advertising Firms in the world. During this time under the instruction of the University of Kentucky, she made a 100 in the class. She graduated with a 3.74 GPA. Dr. June Dawn had dreams of traveling the world for a major corporation, however, after graduation, God stopped her plans and called her back to the ministry.

After submitting 100% to the call of God, she has been serving the Body of Christ in many areas such as websites for pastors, ministries, film, pictures, video, graphic designs, marketing, advertising, etc. She has used her skills to help others. Her heart is to serve the Body of Christ through the direction of the Holy Spirit. Her heart is to continue the servanthood path and help other ministers achieve their destiny as God promotes her to achieve hers. In August 2015, Dr. June Dawn Knight graduated with her Doctorate in Christian Theology at the International Miracle Institute under the direction of Dr. Christian Harfouche and Global Miracle Apostolic Faith Church.

Her Professional VITA:

Dr. June Knight is a specialist on corporate communications, social media, corporations (ministry) media, and communication implementation. Dr. June has served ministries and businesses all over the world to achieve their goals. She partners with leaders and God to obtain the ideal outcome for the vision God placed on the inside of them. Whether it is communicating to a community, a congregation, a nation, or a certain targeted niche, Dr. June helps the visionary to articulate the vision and implement a strategy to obtain maximum effectiveness.

Dr. June's Education:

Bachelor's Degree in Public Relations at Austin Peay State University

Master's Degree in Corporate Communications at APSU

One year of studies at World Harvest Bible College

Doctor of Theology at International Miracle Institute

While in Graduate School at APSU, Dr. June studied in London (Winter 2011/2012) and studied under the top three global marketing/advertising/communication firms in the world. She wrote a 20-page research paper comparing how the United Kingdom markets a product versus the United States. Dr. June completed the class with a grade of 100! Following graduation, Dr. June turned that paper into her first book, Mark of the Beast.

Dr. June has written eleven books. She also is the President and CEO of We are the Bride Ministries which includes: WATB.tv, WATB Radio. She is a TV and Radio Host and is hosting two television shows: BRIDE TIME LIVE and Clarion Call.

Dr. June traveled the entire border of the United States from March 2017 – September 2017, the Lord showed the sickness in the country. In 2018 God showed her the idols in the church and nation then sent her to Washington DC with $9 and a suitcase in 2018. She was there for a year and God did a miracle. She worked in the White House and Secretary of State department in the Press Corps. This is what led to these books.

Manufactured by Amazon.ca
Bolton, ON

13360691R00136